"Your voice has unimaginable power, and you have every right to use it. This book will show you how."

"With candor, wit, and wisdom Ally Henny breaks it all the way down in her debut book, *I Won't Shut Up*. Through an exploration of her life and experiences, Ally offers a glimpse of what it looks like to be your full self in a way that will not be silenced by the racism that often prefers that Black people be neither seen nor heard. *I Won't Shut Up* isn't just about finding your voice but amplifying it to create a more just and inclusive world."

"This book is a love letter to every Black woman and girl who has been told that we are too loud, too angry, too intimidating, too outspoken, too nonconformist, too Black, too feminist . . . too much. Ally Henny draws deep from the well of her own experience to show us that we do not have to silence, shrink, or contort ourselves to fit a world that was never made for us. We can live loud, love loud, and even leave loud."

"Ally Henny has given us a timely gift: a brilliant but humorous prophetic testimony and a road map for freedom in a world that often seeks to silence our voices. For every Black voice that has struggled to speak of freedom, this will loosen up your vocal cords."

"*I Won't Shut Up* is a powerful and bold declaration that reminds us of just how sacred Black women's voices are—especially when they're loud and proud and unapologetic. In her refusal to let white supremacy shut her up, Ally Henny gives us permission to do the same: to not let white supremacy dictate how we live, move, and have our being in this world. This book is a true gift—a guide while on this journey of collective healing and liberation. To those who have ears to hear, let them hear."

Kat Armas, author of *Abuelita Faith* and host of *The Protagonistas* podcast

"Thank God Ally Henny won't shut up. In this honest, provocative book, written in the spirit of liberation and love, she speaks the kind of truth that can set us free. Like the prophets of old, she invites readers to experience transformation, hope, and the possibility of a better future, if only we have the wisdom to listen."

Phil Snider, pastor and editor of *Preaching as Resistance*

I
WON'T
SHUT UP

I WON'T SHUT UP

FINDING YOUR VOICE WHEN THE WORLD TRIES TO SILENCE YOU

ALLY HENNY

BakerBooks

a division of Baker Publishing Group
Grand Rapids, Michigan

© 2023 by Ally Henny

Published by Baker Books
a division of Baker Publishing Group
Grand Rapids, Michigan
www.bakerbooks.com

Printed in the United States of America

Library of Congress Cataloging-in-Publication Data
Names: Henny, Ally, 1985– author.
Title: I won't shut up : finding your voice when the world tries to silence you / Ally Henny.
Other titles: Finding your voice when the world tries to silence you
Description: Grand Rapids, Michigan : Baker Books, a division of Baker Publishing Group, [2023] | Includes bibliographical references.
Identifiers: LCCN 2022040931 | ISBN 9781540902658 (cloth) | ISBN 9781493441150 (ebook)
Subjects: LCSH: Henny, Ally, 1985—Anecdotes. | African women—Biography—Anecdotes. | African Americans—Social conditions—Anecdotes. | Race discrimination—United States—Anecdotes. | Race relations—United States—Anecdotes. | White privilege (Social structure)—United States—Anecdotes. | Prejudices—United States.
Classification: LCC E185.86 .H3647 2023 | DDC 305.896/073—dc23/eng/20221213
LC record available at https://lccn.loc.gov/2022040931

Some names and details have been changed to protect the privacy of the individuals involved.

Published in association with The Bindery Agency, www.TheBinderyAgency.com.

Baker Publishing Group publications use paper produced from sustainable forestry practices and post-consumer waste whenever possible.

23 24 25 26 27 28 29   7 6 5 4 3 2 1

For my Ancestors.
To my descendants.

CONTENTS

Contents

FOREWORD

Danielle Coke

I first came across Ally Henny and her work in a way that you probably can relate to—a witty, honest social media post about the Black experience in white America. She was responding to an incident where a Black woman's work had been stolen by a white woman, and the internet was, justifiably, in an uproar. While Ally's comedic take on the issue drew me in (and had me cackling), it was her persistent pursuit of justice and her dedication to using her voice for the good of others that made me want to stick around.

If there's one thing I've learned after years of being a Black woman and artist speaking out against racism on this wild internet, it's that there is no "right" way to do it that will keep you in the good graces of the white gaze. Whether you're shouting out against injustice in the streets through protest, or you're quietly sitting at home sharing art as a form of digital activism, you will always be too harsh, too aggressive, too intimidating—too loud—for white supremacist culture. In this book, Ally doesn't just want you to face this fact. She wants you to use it as fuel.

Through a collection of personal experiences, careful reflections, and unfiltered truths, Ally is setting us free. On these pages, you will find language that confirms those thoughts you've long held in the back of your mind as you've navigated a justice-focused life as a Black woman, along with a safe space to bring those thoughts out in the open. You will be given tools that you can use right away to keep honing your voice and owning your story. You will be able to rest in the fact that you're not alone and that *your life has always mattered.*

You are about to be taken on a journey through the places that shape us. From the predominantly white spaces that try to rob us of our light to the pews where we are taught that we better let that light shine, Ally reminds us that we are always worthy—even when the winds of white supremacy seek to blow us out.

Here, you won't need to be "resilient" or "strong," but you will need to be brave. Be brave enough to believe that the voices who say you are too much—or not enough—do not get the last word. You don't have to shrink or edit yourself for, as Ally puts it, "Dwight Mahn." Your voice has unimaginable power, and you have every right to use it. This book will show you how.

Ally's words are bold, empowering, and necessary. She is loud on purpose, and through sharing her story with us, she's equipping us to be the same—without apology. As long as racism rears its ugly head in our culture, it will continuously require bold opposition. Rise to the occasion.

Never shut up.

AUTHOR'S NOTE

This book is a work of nonfiction, but it is neither an autobiography, encyclopedia entry, newspaper article, nor courtroom transcript. I have tried to retell the life events contained in this book to the best of my recollection, calling upon old journals, correspondence, and other personal writings to help give me an accurate (if not always precise) account of what happened. In some instances, I have changed names and other identifying information in order to maintain privacy or for narrative clarity. In other instances, I retained names and identifying information so that my work doesn't feel like I'm talking about someone else's life. Occasionally, I combined two or more people, incidents, and/or events to streamline the narrative. I tried to be truthful in everything shared within this book's pages—even when those truths hurt.

As I have written this work, I have worked to prioritize intersectional equity by taking into account various minoritized histories and experiences, and I have tried to use inclusive language. In order for this work to also be readable, I took some shortcuts with language so that my larger point would not get bogged down. There are times where I use "Black," "Black people," or "Black folks" where some iteration of the phrase "people of color" could also fit. Please know that the spirit of this work is inclusivity, even in places where my language isn't as inclusive as it could be.

Additionally, I come to this work as a Black, straight, cisgender, gender-role noncompliant, relatively able-bodied (except for these ankles and knees, Jesus), country-born, city-dwelling, mid-Atlantic informed, Midwest raised, geriatric millennial, Christian woman and with all of the privileges and shortcomings that might accompany those identities and perspectives. I have attempted to do the difficult work of pulling universal truths from my experiences while also attempting to speak to an audience with unique yet overlapping experiences. I don't claim to have done this well, but I gave it my best shot.

Finally, I want to acknowledge and honor the fact that many (if not most) of my readers do not share my Christian spirituality. I want to say up front that the bulk of my adult life and work experience up to this point has been in the Christian church, and so it is an unavoidable fact that parts of my story would be set there. With that said, the church is merely a setting. The truths and wisdom that I pull from the harm that I experienced in the white Christian church are for anyone who wants to be free from racism. Any references to spirituality are for narrative or illustrative purposes; I am not trying to convert you to Christianity.

I hope that this work invites you in and creates space for you to ask questions, wrestle with hard truths, and experience the beauty of healing and liberation.

OVERTURE

Confessions of a Loud Black Woman

I am a loud Black woman.

All of these things are outside of my control, yet I have grappled with each of them in some way for as long as I can remember.

I am a loud Black woman.

I am loud.

I am Black.

I am a woman.

LOUD.

BLACK.

WOMAN.

Each of these identities has been under attack my whole life. Proclaiming my loudness, my Blackness, and my womanness is an act of defiance and resistance. The world continuously tells Black women who we are as if we don't know ourselves. They weaponize our attributes against us, taking the things we celebrate about ourselves and twisting them into something unrecognizable, undesirable, and inadequate. When we are witty, they tell us we are crass or insubordinate. When we display self-confidence, they tell us we are domineering. When we emote, we are told we are exaggerating, angry, or—even worse—threatening.

I refuse to allow the world to force its harsh, dishonest, and out-of-touch definitions on me, which is why I am determined to tell this world exactly who I am. By telling the world who I am, I aim to defy the stereotypes and limitations that society has tried to place on me individually and on Black women collectively. Engaging in self-definition is how I resist the lies that society has tried to tell on loud Black women.

I am a loud Black woman.

Loudness, Blackness, and womanness are considered repulsive by the dominant white male culture. White, straight, cisgender men have made themselves the gold standard, and it is they who dictate how and whether others get to exist in this world. People who hold contested identities regularly find themselves at odds with power structures and systems that were not constructed for their flourishing. These systems are rarely concerned with anything other than protecting and maintaining the status quo of white male dominance. Marginalized folks are expected to act in accordance with this system without resisting. They must push down every part of themselves that doesn't conform to the dictates of the dominant culture. Living in such a world means that it took me a long time to fully own my identity, particularly the loud part.

Society is cruel to Black people, and it doles out a special kind of punishment to *loud* Black people. We can't do ordinary stuff like have a cookout or hang out with our friends without white people hovering over us and trying to place limits on how we express and entertain ourselves. Our mere presence in a space is often all that is needed for us to be perceived as a threat or causing a disturbance, our actual volume notwithstanding. When white people believe that we are disrupting their sense of comfort, which they interpret as us creating a disturbance or posing some type of threat, they try to police us. When we fail to comply with their intrusive attempts to control us and Jump Jim Crow, they will call the actual police to put us in our place. The BBQ Becky incident is the perfect example of this kind of behavior.

In 2018, a white woman named Jennifer Schulte (aka BBQ Becky) called the cops on a group of Black people for having a cookout at a park in Oakland, California, because they were using charcoal in an area that had recently been made off-limits to charcoal grilling. Instead of finding a park ranger—or better yet, minding her business—BBQ Becky resorted to calling 911. Of all the actual emergencies that she could have used William Shatner's three-digit hotline for, she chose to call it on some Negroes who were barbecuing in a park on a sunny day.

One might think that, being in California, Schulte was simply concerned that the charcoal could have sparked a wildfire. Considering California's recent history with fires, one might even be inclined to view her actions as heroic. However, a quick listen to the recordings of Schulte's 911 calls during the incident should be enough to show it ain't that deep. Although Schulte said she was concerned that the "coals" from the barbecue grill could "burn more children," her ultimate motivation was to ensure that her and her fellow gentrifiers' taxes didn't go up.[1] Her concern for kids only extended as far as their protection meant that she didn't have to pay more money in taxes. Put more directly, she was full of crap and gave a full-of-crap explanation to justify her racist actions. A frequent and reliable tactic of toxic whiteness is to use protecting "the children" and not wanting higher taxes as an excuse for racist behavior. White women are particularly adept at using their concern, outrage, and tears as cover for racial wrongdoing and violence.

1. "LISTEN: 'BBQ Becky's' viral 911 call made public," YouTube video, posted by "KTVU FOX 2 San Francisco," August 31, 2018, https://www.youtube.com/watch?v=LgaU1h0QiLo.

If BBQ Becky was actually concerned about the untold danger that used charcoal briquettes posed to society, she could have contacted a park ranger, the fire department, or Smokey the Bear to help her keep her taxes low. Instead, she chose to call the cops, not once but twice, and spend two hours surveilling Black men who were doing nothing more than attempting to have a relaxing time at a public park.

BBQ Becky wasn't out there tryna protect the earth, the children, or even her tax rate. She was doing what white people have tried to do for half a millennium: exercise authority and control over Black people who are doing nothing more than tryna live. When she was met with resistance, she attempted to flip the script and make on like she was the victim—a tactic that is frequently employed by white women seeking to exert power over Black people.

BBQ Becky is proof that being Black and loud in public often draws the voyeuristic eye of white folks who deem themselves to be morally superior and are determined to find a way to shut you up. They will fight, lie, and even fake cry to make sure you regret the moment when you realize that all you have to do in this world is stay Black and die.

Sometimes shutting you up means making an unnecessary call to the cops. Other times it means deciding to take matters into their own hands—which can have a fatal outcome.

For Jordan Davis, a seventeen-year-old boy from Florida, being shut up meant taking several bullets to the chest for listening to loud music. A white man got upset that a group of Black teenagers dared to hang out in a convenience store parking lot, bumping music that he disliked at a volume that he determined was too loud. That white man was sentenced to life in prison. Jordan's parents no longer have their child. Being Black and loud can cost you your life.

Jordan Davis's murder, BBQ Becky, and dozens of similar incidents are exactly why I am not about to let white supremacy tell me that I am too loud. I refuse to accept that I need to tone down my "rhetoric" or shut up. I will not let white supremacy tell my people that we deserve to be harassed, jailed, or killed because our existence makes white people feel uncomfortable. Black people have the right to exist and to take up at least as much space as everybody else. We shouldn't have to adjust ourselves beyond what is required for being a compassionate, ethical person. We shouldn't have to censor, filter, and regulate ourselves while doing ordinary things. We shouldn't have to be afraid that doing everyday stuff might make some white person angry or scared for their lives and so we end up in prison or dead.

A frustrating aspect of white supremacy is that Black people not only have to deal with the white supremacy inflicted on us by white people but we must also contend with other Black folks' internalized white supremacy and anti-Blackness. Respectability politics is one of the main ways that white supremacy shows up when we are amongst ourselves. Respectability politics is the belief that people from a minority group will experience less oppression if they behave in a way that is pleasing to the dominant group, which usually means attempting to imitate the dominant group's ways.

Black people must also cope with white supremacy and anti-Blackness from other racial and ethnic groups. When promoted by non-Black people, respectability politics results in lateral oppression, that is, the harm that marginalized groups enact on one another. In the hands of non-Black people of color, respectability politics becomes a means to reinforce the racial hierarchy that frequently places Black people at the bottom.

Respectability politics tells us to tuck ourselves in and pull our pants up so that white people will treat us with respect and basic human dignity. It tells us that our worth is determined by our level of education, our ability to speak with "good diction," our appearance, and even our ability to avoid being "loud." The fear of harm from white people is real, and respectability politics is a misguided and maladaptive attempt to stay the hand of white wrath. Respectability is a tool of white supremacy because it assumes the inferiority of Black people, our ways, and our culture.

The Black community has always had folks, including some of the Ancestors, who were heavily invested in the notion that assimilation is the key to freedom. We have always had people who connected our oppression to a failure to present ourselves to white people in an "acceptable" manner. It's more than having different preferences from the mainstream of Black culture; engaging in respectability politics involves intentionally distancing oneself from things associated with Blackness out of the misguided assumption that Black people and our culture need fixing or refinement. While these ideas may have served some of our Ancestors' clear and present need for survival, they have done very little for the long-term flourishing of the Black community.

To be clear, I give the Ancestors all of their roses for the work that they did for us. I would not be writing this book if it weren't for the sacrifices of women like Ida B. Wells, Fannie Lou Hamer, and my personal hero, Ella Baker. Not all of the Ancestors were down with respectability politics (the women I just mentioned weren't), but the influence of respectability politics on our discourse and freedom-seeking efforts is undeniable. The Ancestors did what they felt they had to do in order to survive in their time. Adhering to the politics of respectability was one of those things. We can celebrate our Ancestors' accomplishments while also acknowledging the long-term negative impact that some of their ideas have had on our community. It is important for those of us who are alive in this day and age to recognize just how messed up it was that our Ancestors had to demonstrate their humanity to white people by attempting to act like them.

Respectability politics is a tool of white supremacy, and we should want no part of it. We can't be out here doing the work of white supremacy as if we aren't still contending with actual white supremacists. Sadly, there are some Black people who are intent on doing the work of white supremacy because they are not yet free enough to see that respectability is a concept that doesn't deliver what it promises. Everybody has a journey that they must walk of liberating themselves from white supremacy and internalized racism. Fighting for freedom means fighting for people who don't yet realize that they need to be free.

Respectability politics don't save us. Being a professor at Harvard didn't save Henry Louis Gates from having the cops called on him when he tried to get into his own house. Being rich didn't stop someone from telling Oprah that she couldn't look at a handbag. Being a worship leader at a church didn't save Botham Jean from being shot to death in his own apartment. Being a SigRho didn't stop Sandra Bland from dying in jail after getting picked up for a traffic offense. Being a football player at an HBCU didn't stop the cops from shooting Jonathan Ferrell twelve times. Respectability politics won't save us.

What respectability does is steal from us. It steals our esteem for who we are as Black people and replaces it with a sense of shame. It makes us ashamed of our communities. It makes us ashamed of our vernacular. It makes us ashamed of our culture—the food, art, beliefs, and everything else that makes Blackness unique. It makes us ashamed of any aspect of our culture that doesn't jibe with the mandates of whiteness. It even makes us ashamed of one another.

One of the first things that respectability politicians will say about other Black folks is that they are loud, and they will make sure everybody knows that they prefer to carry themselves in a more dignified manner. They will express disdain for certain Black celebrities they say are loud. They won't watch certain Black shows or listen to certain types of Black music because they associate them with loudness. They won't dress in certain clothing styles because they are too loud.

Respectability politics usually defines loudness as any attribute, attitude, or action that is not carried out in a subdued or understated manner. On this wise, loudness isn't necessarily determined by volume, though volume is part of what is considered loud. Loudness, essentially, is drawing attention to oneself by breaking certain social norms. There is a strong element of subjectivity to loudness; what is deemed loud in one setting is not necessarily considered loud in other circumstances. Social class, education, and geographic location often determine what people might deem loud. Generally, what people call loud is considered loud because it trends away from what is considered normal by the dominant, white culture.

It is no small coincidence that what respectability politics tells us is loud is also what is looked down upon by white society. White society takes issue with loudness. In white culture, loudness is associated with being uncouth, which is why virtually any place that white culture esteems as a paragon of sophistication and taste is quiet, if not totally silent. Museums, orchestra concerts, theatre productions, and high-end restaurants are just a few of the places where white culture demands restraint—if not absolute silence—from its patrons.

White culture associates loudness with being uneducated, un-cultured, and poor. This is why a lot of white comedians, especially those of the blue-collar variety, are loud and bawdy. By embracing the speaking volume of the working class, they push the aesthetic boundaries of whiteness. It's not that loud white people don't exist, because they do, but being a loud white person is not seen so much as a problem to be eliminated as it is an attribute in need of refinement. The behavior of loud whites is rarely regulated and is often seen as a negligible quality of a group of people who carry a certain provincial charm. In other words, whiteness confers the privilege of loudness on poor white people.

Poor white people get to be loud because their whiteness shields them from being seen as a threat, and, if anything, their loudness is viewed as an endearing quality that comes with their social status. White loudness is nonthreatening and entertaining to other white people, and if there is anything that middle- and upper-class white people love, it is to be entertained by working-class white folks. They enjoy laughing at the expense of poor white folks almost as much as they love being entertained by Black people. Middle-class white people get to laugh at and be entertained by the loud, poor white folks. The poor white folks get to feel seen by society, all the while laughing at themselves to keep from crying about their marginalized status in the white power structure.

The one shred of hope, the singular bone that the white bourgeois throws to poor white people is that, if they maintain white solidarity, they will never be treated as badly as Black, Indigenous, and Brown folks. A sordid detail of the whiteness conspiracy is that poor whites have always been eager to trade their dignity for a semblance of power over people of color. It was poor white people who were the overseers and enforcers on the plantation during slavery. It was poor white people who carried out America's colonization agenda that led to the genocide of Indigenous peoples. And it was poor white people who seemed to be the most stirred up about Brown people immigrating to the United States from other parts of the world after September 11, 2001, and who chanted "build the wall" during the 2016 election cycle.

White people can keep their loudness as long as it serves the purposes of whiteness and follows its dictates. Everyone else must shut up or be shut up.

I refuse to let white supremacy shut me up.

I am a loud Black woman.

You don't have to allow white supremacy to shut you up either. You have permission to be as loud as you want to.

When we claim our loudness, we flout the standards that the dominant culture tries to impose upon people who are loud, particularly and especially Black women. Being Black comes with the assumption that you are being loud no matter what your actual volume is. Beyond one's speaking volume, loudness is drawing more attention or taking up more space than white people—or Black folks who are doing the work of white supremacy—think you should. Natural hairstyles are loud. Wigs and weaves are loud. Long fingernails are loud. Curvy hips and a full bosom are loud. Speaking slang is loud. Speaking "standard" English is loud. Wearing a dashiki is loud. Wearing high heels is loud. Being athletic is loud. Being fat is loud. Having a GED is loud. Having a PhD is loud. Being on welfare is loud. Making six figures is loud. Existing is loud.

It seems like no matter what Black women do, whatever our choices are, we are seen as loud. And our loudness is perceived as anger, whether we're actually angry or not. Whiteness uses Black women's anger against us as a way to disqualify and discredit us because the dominant culture can only hear those who speak in syrupy sweet tones. And since our very existence has been labeled as loud and angry, our very existence is also thoroughly discredited and disqualified. Therefore, Black women must shut up or be shut up.

Black women are told to shut up because our existence in this world loudly testifies that no one should be forced to fit inside other people's boxes. Try as we might, our bodies do not easily bend to white standards of beauty. As much as our bodies refuse to bend to white norms, our spirits also refuse to be broken by them. We are the daughters of women who survived the slave master's whip and the colonizer's gun. Many of us are the offspring of women who endured and survived the harshness of the Middle Passage. We carry the burdens and the traumas of our foremothers within our own bodies. We come from women who fought to survive, many of them trusting in their God to "make a way outta no way" when the white man tried to convince them that their only value was found on their backs and between their thighs.

As much as whiteness tries to invalidate, erase, and ignore Black women, still we rise. As much as whiteness attempts to silence us, we keep making noise in stereo. Individually, our loudness has allowed us to push back against our oppression. Collectively, our loudness has supported and carried the cause of Black freedom both within and outside of the Black community.

For me to claim and proclaim the fact that I am a loud Black woman is to dismantle the oppression that comes with carrying these identities. But before I get too deep into proclaiming and dismantling, I should tell you a bit about how being a loud Black woman has shaped who I am. I wasn't always as outspoken about my loudness, my Blackness, or my womanness. Finding my voice in a world that constantly tells Black women we are too loud was hard.

I have had to fight to get to where I am, and that is what this book is about.

I hope that, as you read this book, you will find yourself in my story. I hope that as you find yourself in my story, you will also find your voice. I hope that finding your voice will help you to speak the truth. And I hope that the truth will set you free.

ACT I

THE (NOT SO) SECRET ORIGINS OF ALLY HENNY

1

A WALKING CONTRADICTION

*Learning to Lay Down the Burden
of White Supremacy*

I am a walking contradiction of sorts.

I am loud, but I am also shy. Very shy. *Painfully* shy.

People who have known me for any length of time are often surprised to find this out about me because in situations that require me to be "on," I can be quite loud and animated without giving the slightest hint that I am feeling apprehensive. In small groups or one-on-one, I can be quite talkative—if I am comfortable around you or if you ask me the right questions.

I have a loud voice. I have worked very hard over the years to develop a range of volume, but my normal speaking voice is usually fairly loud. I chalk it up to growing up in a large, loud extended family—I am actually one of the quieter ones. I also have a loud, ugly, and extra laugh. I laugh extra and have the audacity to love to laugh. When I laugh, I scream, wheeze, clap, stomp, fall out, jump, cry, cough, shake, dance, and Lord knows what else. I can be in a room by myself and have a thought pop into my head and I'll start laughing uncontrollably and have tears running down my face. In fact, I'm laughing as I write this thinking about how I just be laughing at something that I can't explain to other people because I can't talk about it without laughing.

A lot of people conflate loudness with extroversion and assume that since I'm loud, I must also be an extrovert. This couldn't be farther from the truth. I am an introvert, but after I warm up to a situation and have the opportunity to talk about something I'm passionate about, I will talk long and very loudly about it. The truth is, I would rather try to brush an alligator's teeth than be in a social situation with people I don't know. I have spent many a restless night worrying about what I was going to say and how I was going to act in a new social setting. I'm always grateful when a close friend or relative is able to be with me in a new environment so I can figuratively "hide behind" them—I would literally hide if I could.

The complicated fears, concerns, and emotions that I feel in a new social situation make it hard for me to find my words at first. I need time to get my bearings and read the room before I can come out of my shell. I don't think my shyness is serious enough to be considered full-blown social anxiety, but it is enough that I often feel nervous and have to prepare myself for possible interactions with people by reviewing my "social script," which is nothing more than a few generic interactions I run through in my mind to remind myself of how to talk to people.

Having a social script is a skill that my mom taught me, and it has served me well throughout my life. My natural, unrefined impulse when I walk into a new situation is to put my head down and wait to be seen or acknowledged, but my mom taught me to hold my head high and engage with the space that I'm in. Thanks to her coaching from childhood to college, I've been told by many different people that I often command attention when I enter a room.

If I could articulate how I manage to fool people into thinking I am a commanding and confident person, I would market it and make a bunch of money. Perhaps the secret is having a Black mother who asks, "What do you say when you walk into a room?" every morning as you stumble half asleep into the bathroom with a full bladder that needs to be relieved, but you have to stop and say, "Good morning," before you can plop down and squeeze out a drop.

Still, I spend a lot of time worrying and wondering if my mouth is doing justice to the ideas and observations that I feel so confident about when they live in my mind. I worry and wonder if my words, my gestures, my body, and my voice are taking up too much space.

I love hearing other people's thoughts, and I love sharing my thoughts and exchanging ideas. I just have to get past the initial wave of shyness that comes first. I have been this way for as long as I can remember.

When I was five years old, my mom took me to see Miss Estelle at Headhunters Salon for my first relaxer. Miss Estelle was a white woman who knew how to do Black people's hair: a precious commodity in a small, predominantly white town. If you were a Black woman in my little rural Missouri town, you either did your hair yourself or you depended on friends and relatives to do your hair in their kitchen salons. If you wanted professional quality perms, cuts, or styles, you drove the two hours to Kansas City to get your hair done at one of the Black beauty shops there. Of course, going to the city to get your hair done meant that it was a half-day, if not an all-day, affair—not to mention gas money and salon prices—which is why it was a big deal when a white woman who claimed she could do Black hair set up shop locally.

As we drove up to the shop, I took extra notice of its sign. It was black and had "Headhunters Salon" painted on it in bamboo-style letters, and there was a picture of a person sitting in a cauldron with another person looming over them. I would never patronize a place with such a politically incorrect and demeaning sign today, but it was the early 1990s in rural Missouri and this kind of problematic kitsch was—and still is—everywhere. I had seen this sign countless times, but I suddenly became aware of its implications. I couldn't read the name of the salon, but I had seen enough Bugs Bunny cartoons to understand that sitting down in a cauldron could be bad news. I instantly became wary of what might be taking place inside.

I was relieved to learn, upon entering the salon, that I would be sitting in a chair and not a cauldron full of hot water. That still didn't allay the nervousness I felt. I was nervous about getting my hair done (it was my first time in a salon, after all), but I was also nervous because I didn't know Miss Estelle.

"Have a seat," Miss Estelle said, swiveling the black chair in my direction. We were the only people in the big, empty salon. Although I was tall for my age, I felt very small among the chairs, sinks, and hair dryers that multiplied into infinity in the mirrors that surrounded us.

I climbed into the chair and was surprised when it started inching its way upward as Miss Estelle pumped the metal bar at its base, the clunky sound of metal and air echoing through the beauty shop. I felt forty feet tall when the chair came to a stop, leaving me almost face-to-face with Miss Estelle. She covered me in a large grayish-black cape and fastened it in the back.

"Too tight?" she asked.

I shook my head, my eyes dropping to the nylon shroud enveloping my body.

As Miss Estelle took my hair out of the four large, puffy, two-strand twists that were my usual style, she asked my mom some questions about my hair. There was a large mirror that went across the opposite wall. I would occasionally lift my eyes from the spot that I was staring at on the cape to look at myself and watch Mom talk to Miss Estelle. After confirming what she wanted Miss Estelle to do to my hair, Mom left me at the salon.

"How old are you?" Miss Estelle turned the chair to one side and gave it one last pump.

"Five," I replied, my eyes still fixed on my cape.

"Do you go to school?" she asked, donning a pair of plastic gloves.

I nodded.

"Can you lift your head up for me?"

I realized that my head had dropped almost all the way down, and my chin was practically buried in the salon cape. I lifted my head and Miss Estelle started to section my hair. There was some tugging and occasional discomfort, but she was much gentler with my head than Mom usually was, so I didn't complain.

Every time Miss Estelle asked me a question, my cheeks felt hot and prickly as I replied. But her voice was warm and inviting, so I began to feel at ease. Soon my replies got longer and longer until I didn't need her questions anymore. The next thing I knew, I was telling Miss Estelle everything I knew about the Teenage Mutant Ninja Turtles and any other subject that came to mind.

I talked as she applied the relaxer.

I talked as she washed the relaxer out.

I talked as I sat under the hair dryer.

I talked when it was time to go back to the salon chair for styling.

I talked as my mom returned to the salon to collect me.

"I didn't think that she would say very much, but she talked *the whole time*." Miss Estelle chuckled.

Unfazed, Mom replied with her usual speech. "She can talk. She talks so much that I have to tell her that I need a break sometimes. She even talks herself to sleep."

Mom and Miss Estelle exchanged a laugh.

I felt a little sheepish for talking so much.

Coming from a family of extroverts, I learned early how to navigate the expectations of people who don't always understand introverts. My elders used to chide me over my facial expressions because they were concerned that people would think I was angry. I wasn't angry; I was just so deep in thought that my brow furrowed and my jaw hardened. Their criticism hurt because I wanted to be left alone without the burden of managing others' perceptions of me.

I eventually came to understand why my elders always seemed so critical of me. They were teaching me how to survive in a world that is harsh to Black women. I don't know if they would have articulated their motives in this exact way, but the principle was clear. Black women can't afford to give a bad impression because we may never be given the chance to make up for it. We must remain vigilant about the messages we telegraph to others and be mindful about what others might think they see in us.

My grandma, mom, and aunties all grew up under the white gaze during Jim Crow and the Civil Rights Movement in a rural Missouri town that was just as small and white as where I was raised. Although they lived in other places at various points, a significant portion of their lives were spent in places that were constructed to cater to the sensibilities of whiteness. They were not trying to be hurtful as much as they were trying to pass down the hard-won knowledge that they and our Ancestors had gained along the way. They were teaching me how to live in a world where Black women don't always get to explain ourselves. They were teaching me how to survive in a society that polices our every move—right down to our facial expressions.

People act as if Black women are not entitled to privacy; we must always be fit for public consumption. And when we're seen as unfit, well, it's all the more reason for white people to whip us into shape. Of course, they used to use actual whips, but since they can't do that anymore, they've found other ways to beat us into submission.

When we go about our business without feeling the need to smile every second, we're told that we have resting bitch face—a term with both sexist and racist implications when it is applied to Black women. They will call us bitches outright when we are emotionally reserved and don't put all of our business and feelings out on Front Street the way white women do. If it's a white church setting, they'll sanctify it by calling us "unapproachable," which is just white church folks' way of calling us the b-word.

If you ask hard questions and refuse to accept half-baked answers, they'll call you a troublemaker. If you hold people accountable for their actions and refuse to shut up until you're satisfied, they'll call you pushy and insubordinate. If you don't accept their tone policing and their attempts to exert control over how you conduct yourself in public, they'll call you uncooperative. If you don't allow yourself to be pushed around, they'll call you unteachable and uncoachable. When you refuse to be their beast of burden, they'll tell you that you're not a team player. When you set boundaries, they'll call your dedication into question.

Black women don't get no rest.

The only thing that Black women in white spaces get to be is On. On call. On guard. On point. On mission. On message. Always On. Never off. Never off-beat. Never off-kilter. Never off-brand. Never off-balance. Never off-putting.

Never off.

Always On.

As a Black woman who is talkative in some instances and more reserved in others, I have frequently been the subject of white suspicion and insecurity. White people have constructed entire narratives about me because I wasn't talkative when they thought that I ought to be. They chose to believe that I was angry, stuck-up, unhelpful, or had a chip on my shoulder when I was just chillin'. Being Black and an introvert means that white people frequently read your introversion as a threat.

White culture's concept of Black people is the "happy Blacks" who are always smiling, singing a song, and ready to entertain—as long as we're not too loud while doing it. We are to be available to them at all times. White people don't know what to do with themselves when they encounter a Black person, especially a Black woman, who is emotionally reserved and quiet. They think that everything is by, for, and about them, and so they perceive an introverted Black woman's placid demeanor as a personal slight. Her reservedness must be because she is angry at an individual white person, or even worse, because she hates white people in general. Her silence is because she is angry, plotting, and has a bad attitude that needs to be brought into order.

I've had more than my fair share of run-ins with white individuals who were all up in their feelings because they took my introversion as a personal affront. I have had to reassure them that I am not mad at them or stewing over some interaction they insist must've upset me even though I can't remember anything about it. I have had to explain that I am an introvert who might be talkative sometimes and more reserved other times and that it has nothing to do with them and everything to do with the fact that I can't be On all the time. I shouldn't have to explain myself, but sometimes an explanation is the only thing that will ward off the danger that comes with white people's suspicion and hurt feelings.

I've also had more than my fair share of run-ins with white folks who were all up in their feelings because they took my loudness as a personal affront. I have experienced emotional outbursts from people who were angry that I was knowledgeable and confident when they expected me to be ignorant and deferential to them. I have been guilt-tripped for displaying competence and leadership. I have had people treat me as if I were volatile and could say or do something wrong and extremely destructive at any moment. I have been told I should stay in my place and not talk about things that make them feel uncomfortable.

I used to beat myself up for being a walking contradiction because it always seemed to lead to others misunderstanding me. I hate being misunderstood. There have been moments when it felt like I could do nothing to suit anyone. I couldn't trust my instincts because they would lead to a hard conversation with someone I had managed to frustrate or disappoint in some way. I obsessed over how to stand, how loud to talk, when to make eye contact, when to let someone be wrong, and when to stand up for what I believed was right. I tried so hard to lock myself inside of others' boxes that, for a minute, I lost myself.

But I came back to myself when I realized that, while some of my hang-ups and life issues were the result of a need for personal growth, I was also carrying burdens placed upon me by white supremacy. What I had to learn is that being loud or quiet doesn't actually matter. White people will find some kind of fault with you and use it as a reason to treat you as less than. When you assimilate in one area, they'll find something else that needs to be fixed. When you try to do right, they will find something wrong about it.

Black women don't get no rest.

When I was growing up, my family attended a little Baptist church that sat on the edge of what some of the Elders called Black End, which was where most of the Black people in my hometown lived until we were allowed to buy houses in the other parts of town. Most weeks, we sang an old spiritual that went:

> Glory, glory, hallelujah!
> Since I laid my burdens down.
> Glory, glory, hallelujah!
> Since I laid my burdens down!

My grandma and other elders in the church would clap and "get happy" as they sang this song. I would listen to them, half terrified because I couldn't understand why they would suddenly cry out or have a "Baptist fit" and half amused because people catching the Holy Ghost is some of the only entertainment that Black church kids get in a three-hour-long service.

Now that I'm grown, I understand why the Elders used to "get happy" singing about laying their burdens down. Black folks traverse a world that places heavy burdens on our backs, and there aren't many places where we get to lay those burdens down. Singing about laying down the weight the world placed on them gave my Elders the strength they needed to keep on keepin' on.

We can learn so much from the simple wisdom found in our Elders' and Ancestors' commitment to freedom. They understood what it meant to live in a world where they were constantly disrespected and mistreated. They understood what it was like to feel constant pressure to do right so the worst manifestations of white supremacy wouldn't be visited upon them. We can use some of the tools they gave us to facilitate our own liberation. For some of us, that might mean leaning into our spirituality and catching the Holy Ghost at an altar in a Black church while laying our burdens at the feet of Jesus. For others, freedom might come in the form of a group chat where we lean into our chosen community to help lighten the load.

Through racialized oppression and violence, society has conditioned Black folks, particularly Black women, to be burden bearers. We often make accommodations without realizing it because life has taught us that we have to bend over backward like Neo in *The Matrix* in order to avoid being harmed by racism. We spend years cultivating a "professional" demeanor by tamping down our personalities so that we can avoid the Angry Black Woman stereotype. We work extra hard to make sure white folks feel comfortable around us so that our directness isn't coded as unfriendliness. We fear being too loud, and so we shut up.

What would happen if, instead of accepting burden-bearing and making accommodations for everyone but ourselves, we chose self-acceptance? What would happen if, instead of trying to compensate for our perceived shortcomings, we embraced our contradictions?

For many years, I thought that I had to bear the burden of oppression silently, alone, and with a smile on my face. I started to get free when I realized that I am not alone. *You* are not alone. There are others, like you, who want to come out of silence and be set free. You don't have to be shackled by the heavy burdens that society places on your back. You can lay those burdens down. You don't have to bear indignity while wearing a smile. You have the power to talk back to injustice.

Unfortunately, talking back is sometimes easier to talk about than it is to do. A lot of us received messaging, from an early age even, that we could not talk back to people who exert power over us. Sometimes this messaging was reinforced with punishment or abuse. We've been programmed to associate talking back with negative consequences, and so we struggle to speak up in the face of injustice out of fear of retribution.

When it comes to talking back to racial injustice, the risk of retribution is real. History shows us that white supremacy will inflict violence upon Black people when we challenge its power. History also shows us that freedom comes when Black people talk back to injustice. Our Ancestors didn't shut up. You don't have to shut up either.

I didn't come out of the womb fighting injustice. It took time for me to recognize the devastating impact that injustice can bring into our lives and to decide to push back. It took time for me to find my voice. My desire to live in a just world arose as a result of receiving messages that made me question my worth and experiencing things that left me feeling powerless. It took years for me to learn to accept myself and lay my burdens down, but now that I've found my voice, I feel better. So much better. You can feel better too. It's time to lay those burdens down.

> I feel better, so much better
> Since I laid my burdens down.
> I feel better, so much better
> Since I laid my burdens down!

2

THE CONSTELLATION
OF HARMS

*Understanding the Interconnectedness
of Injustice*

My mom has an ancient VHS tape somewhere of my sister and me standing in the bathroom after bath time. It begins with the sound of weeping and wailing and gnashing of teeth (all coming from me) and Amy, my big sister, trying to calm me down. Amy is twelve years older than me, and so she was often put in charge of my baths. During this particular bath time, I had become upset because Amy was, to quote four-year-old me, "putting words in my mouth."

I'm not entirely sure what behooved our mom to pull out our seventy-five-pound camcorder to document this event, but there she was, standing in the doorway, conducting an interview that could rival any Barbara Walters special. Over the course of the vignette, we find out that I was trying to say something of great importance—what that was exactly has been lost to history—but Amy kept "putting words in my mouth." That is, she kept trying to finish my sentences for me, and I was not here for it. At one point in the video Amy, whose back was to my mom, turned around and gave the camera the same side-eye that would later be immortalized by Stanley Hudson on *The Office*.

From childhood into young adulthood, I struggled with a cycle of self-consciousness, embarrassment, and even shame around using my voice. When I was little, my grandma used to tell me that I was "talking [her] head off," which was the second most common thing she said to me besides, "Your mouth goes like a bell clapper." I was an adult before I realized what a bell clapper was (it's the thing that makes a bell ring), and I still don't know how to feel about the comparison, however apt it may be. I can laugh about such comparisons now, but there was a time when how I talked, the amount that I talked, and what people thought of my talking made me feel terribly self-conscious.

A lot of my early insecurity about using my voice stemmed from a fear of not being heard or not being taken seriously. I am the baby of my nuclear family, and I was the baby girl of my extended family for a long time. I was raised with and by my extended family, and so my aunties, uncles, big cousins, and grandma all had a hand in my upbringing. I was a precocious and intellectually curious kid, and there were times when I would say things that surprised or amused the grownups in my life, and they would laugh about it. I would feel frustrated because I wasn't being taken seriously so I would try harder to get them to take me seriously and they would laugh even more.

I don't think that my grandma, mom, and the rest of my family were ever intentionally condescending toward me, but no matter the intention, it still produced insecurity within me.

As I grew from childhood into my preteen years, my family's patience with my verbosity started to thin. A lot of it had to do with the fact that my grandmother, the matriarch and solid rock of our family, was in progressively failing health. When I was five, Grandma went into atrial fibrillation at my Aunt Sue's house. Sue, a registered nurse, had to perform CPR on her until the ambulance came. From that point forward, my mom and aunts made sure that Grandma was never by herself for very long and that my cousins and I knew what to do in the event of an emergency.

This training would be put to good use six years later when Grandma had a stroke not long after my cousins and I had gotten off the school bus. The four of us sprang into action, calling 911, asking one of the neighbors to come over, and caring for our baby cousin who was barely a year old at the time. Our heroic efforts, and the fact that Grandma was administered a new, life-saving drug when she arrived at the hospital, were covered on the Kansas City news.

Not long after the stroke, Grandma was diagnosed with lung cancer. She had been a heavy smoker until her A-fib episode, and the doctors had been monitoring a spot on her lung for several years. For whatever reason, that spot became larger after the stroke, and she entered into radiation treatments in an attempt to stop the cancer's progress. For a little more than a year, my whole family banded together to help take care of Grandma. My cousin Staci and I, being the two oldest of the five grandchildren who were in my grandmother's care while our parents worked, learned how to cook and manage household chores. Kendall and Kameron, my younger twin cousins, helped take care of baby Dominique and helped Grandma any way they could. No one told us that we had to do these things; we did them because it was the right thing to do.

Cancer isn't fair. It doesn't give a damn about your feelings. It doesn't give a damn about your plans or your free time. It doesn't give a damn that the medicine that's supposed to prolong your life also makes you irritable. It doesn't give a damn about giving you so much pain that all you can do is sit with your eyes closed, praying that the pain will pass. It doesn't give a damn about your family. It doesn't give a damn about anybody or anything.

Cancer isn't fair.

From the great injustice of cancer sprang many others—like streams from a mighty river. For that season, everything was focused on Grandma and her health, and everyone, including Grandma, was stressed and their emotions were on a hair trigger. The rawness of everyone's emotions meant that some of the smallest issues became magnified. I often found myself on the wrong side of these issues, and my desire to be heard and taken seriously only made things worse. It was out of the fires of this trial that my keen sense of justice was refined.

Part of Grandma's care was regular visits by a nurse. One day, when the nurse arrived, Staci, Kendall, Kameron, and I were playing a game in the front yard. It didn't take long for us to start whooping, hollering, and carrying on as our game became increasingly competitive.

Suddenly, Grandma's frail figure framed the glass storm door with black wrought iron bars, and we heard the familiar creak that let us know we were about to receive some sort of instruction, rebuke, or combination of both. Grandma mumbled something, and I noticed that Kameron and Staci—who were in position to hear her better than I could—started heading toward the front steps. I realized that we had been told to come inside.

We were having fun, and I was reluctant to go into the house. Although the sun was setting, there was still plenty of light outside. I assumed that, since the nurse was there, we were being asked to come inside because we were either being too noisy or Grandma thought that we weren't getting along. I told her that we weren't arguing and tried to convince her to let us keep playing outside. As Grandma and I went back and forth, the rest of the kids obediently sat down on the sofa in the living room. I huffed and sat down also, still trying to convince Grandma to let us go back outside. The other kids were silent. The nurse looked on, her head turning back and forth between Grandma and me as if she were watching a tennis match.

The whole thing felt completely unfair. It wasn't fair that Grandma's nerves were bad and so we had to come inside while we were having so much fun. It wasn't fair that she wasn't giving us a reason for why we had to stop playing. It wasn't fair that we had to sit in the living room, without the TV on, and listen to Grandma and the nurse talk about boring grownup stuff when we could have been enjoying ourselves outside. This was just one more unfair thing to add to the pile of crappy and unfair stuff that was happening. I was hurt and frustrated because nobody seemed to care about how unfair it was except for me.

A day or two after the incident, I found out that the nurse told one of my family members that I had "sassed" Grandma when we were told to come inside, and that the nurse had "seen a side" of me that she had "never seen before." The saga was eventually recounted to Mom and the other grownups, who were horrified by my behavior.

I tried to explain myself, but no one wanted to listen. They were all shocked and angry that I would behave in a way that could have jeopardized Grandma's health, and they were disappointed that my behavior reflected poorly on my character and our family. I felt humiliated, misunderstood, and ashamed. I wasn't trying to be disrespectful, and I certainly didn't want Grandma to get sicker or die because she had used up all her strength arguing with me. The more I tried to convince everyone of my intent and that the entire situation was unfair, the more I felt like the villain of the story. I realize now that I wasn't the villain; cancer was.

It's not like I never got to play or do anything fun—my childhood is full of such happy memories—but in that particular moment, it felt like something that was hard for me to name was being taken away. I realize now that I was feeling the weight of all of the smaller injustices that had stacked up and were bearing down on me.

Injustice often creates what I refer to as a "constellation of harms." Harm can be understood as a physical, social, psychological, or emotional injury that results from individual, collective, or societal wrongdoing, whether such wrongdoing is intentional or unintentional. A constellation of harms consists of a network of interconnected and often interdependent sources of harm that constitute or exacerbate a larger injustice. Like the stars in a constellation, some harms may be larger or more visible, while others are less perceptible but still present. Sometimes a series of smaller harms contributes to a larger injustice. Other times a larger injustice creates a series of smaller harms.

We often don't perceive a constellation of harms because we struggle to recognize the relationship between various harms and injustices. We might be able to discern immediate cause and effect relationships, but we struggle to connect effects to causes that are farther removed from the initial incident. Like the stars in the night sky, the constellations are only visible if you know what you're looking for. But once you know what you're looking at, the night sky never looks the same.

Injustice is rarely an isolated affair. Larger injustices create smaller harms that, in turn, feed back into larger injustices. The system goes back and forth, around and around, while compounding on itself until entropy threatens to propel us into a vast black hole of injustice. As injustice compounds in the world, it can make those of us who are justice-minded feel like we're being swallowed up into the vastness of outer space. Pushing back can sometimes feel like shouting into the void, but I firmly believe that there's truth in the aphorism "the arc of the moral universe is long, but it bends toward justice."[1]

***

As my universe started to bend in the wake of Grandma's cancer diagnosis, I felt myself being catapulted into the vastness of outer space, my body flying through the stars mapping out my own constellation of harms. As I attempted to push back, to propel myself back to planet Earth, Injustice shouted from the abyss, "Who do you think you are?" When I told Injustice exactly who I was, it responded by calling me outside my name. When I pleaded with Injustice to call me by my name, it tried to steal my voice from me. It tried to convince me that I didn't have a story, that my words had no value. But when I talked back to Injustice, I noticed that it seemed to lose some of its power. I noticed that my words could fill the emptiness of outer space with water and air and that I could travel back to Earth on the sound waves that my voice created.

So I talked back.

I argued.

I pointed out any and everything that I saw that was unfair in my world.

Injustice had tried to stifle my voice, but it didn't anticipate that its very existence only made my voice stronger. It would be years before I would start to recognize and come into my power, but Injustice had sown the wind and in time it would reap the whirlwind.

1. Martin Luther King Jr., "Remaining Awake Through a Great Revolution," in *A Testament of Hope: The Essential Writings and Speeches of Martin Luther King, Jr.*, ed. James Melvin Washington (1986, repr., San Francisco: Harper-Collins, 1991), 277.

Recognizing that Grandma's cancer contributed to a constellation of harms has helped me properly grieve her sickness, loss, and all of the difficult moments it produced for my family and me. I used to be hard on myself for how I acted and felt during those years, but time and distance have helped me see that everyone was just trying to do their best in a difficult situation. Although I wish that I hadn't had to watch Grandma live with such a terrible illness and that I would have had her longer than twelve all-too-short years, I have come to make peace with it. My grandmother's illness made me acutely aware of and sensitive to the existence of injustice in the world. Losing her how and when I did made me who I am today.

Understanding injustice as a constellation of harms allows us to pull it out of the realm of individual experience and recognize its broader impact on everyone. Individualism and toxic positivity minimize humanity's interconnectedness and block us from fully perceiving the impact of injustice by reducing it to individualized misfortunes that can be rehabilitated into teachable moments and triumph narratives. Freedom becomes dependent on an individual's ability to "overcome adversity," but that ain't real freedom. A turd dipped in gold and studded with diamonds is still a turd. Freedom isn't a reward issued to those who are able to withstand mistreatment and endure hardship; it is our birthright and shouldn't have to be earned. Positivity isn't what sets us free; it is the truth that sets us free by forcing us to confront the ugliness and brutality we see in the world.

American society's addiction to rugged individualism and toxic positivity has resulted in an inability to name and adequately reckon with injustice. Individualism twists adversity and harm into isolated incidents and makes the outcome of such incidents the sole responsibility of the person experiencing them. When people experience harm, there is pressure to quickly "get over" what happened and find some kind of happy ending that ties everything up in a perfect bow and places it on a shelf not to be remarked on again (except to talk about how "beautiful" the situation ended up being). What we're left with is a broader culture that understands very little about collective harm, collective grief, collective injustice, and our collective responsibility to build a just world. This often leads to a shallow understanding of the impact that injustice has on individuals and on society.

People want to believe that they are solely a product of their own choices, but the reality is that we are a product of our choices *and* others' decisions. We are a product of our own actions *and* the cumulative actions of others in society. We are individuals inasmuch as we are part of collective humanity. Recognizing that injustice consists of a constellation of harms allows us to see its collective nature.

American society's struggle to understand the collective nature of injustice also has implications on the way we understand ourselves in relation to racial inequity.

White supremacy weaponizes toxic positivity against racially marginalized people by convincing us that we are somehow to blame for the constellation of harms emanating from present and historical wrongdoing. This racist toxic positivity culture goads us into believing that there is a prize for never saying a mumblin' word while bearing our burdens. It reinforces survivor's bias by convincing people who have managed to overcome obstacles that shouldn't exist in the first place that they possess the heroic traits of "pluckiness" and "grit" that allowed them to "beat the odds." These survivors often become some of the most ardent proponents of toxic positivity culture as they admonish others not to have a "poverty mindset" and unwittingly accept assimilation and cultural erasure. They see themselves as giving back or sharing wisdom with their communities, but they end up inadvertently reinforcing white supremacist narratives about Black folks.

Identifying our own constellation of harms is one of the initial steps in the journey of finding our voice in the face of injustice. This isn't a navel-gazing, woe-is-me exercise. Identifying our own constellation of harms empowers us to seek justice from a place of authority and conviction. You may not be an expert on education, economics, or the law, but you are the expert on your own lived experience.

You have the power to name your experiences and evaluate how those experiences fit into broader social narratives. For example, around the same time that my grandma was receiving treatment for lung cancer, Big Tobacco was facing a reckoning. It was all over the news that the tobacco companies had covered up what they had known all along about the health risks of smoking. Not long after her diagnosis, I heard Grandma tell a family friend, "I smoked for fifty years, and now I wished that I hadn't never started."

Although it was my grandmother's choice to start smoking, the forces of capitalism and corporate greed ensured that she would continue using a product that was harmful. She was only able to stop after the damage had long been done. The constellation of harms that impacted my grandma's health would soon come to affect me as I had experiences during her illness that impact me to this day. The corporate greed of Big Tobacco isn't responsible for all the problems in my life, but the constellation of harms stemming from their greed certainly left its mark.

Identifying our constellation of harms is critical to the work of liberation. We cannot experience freedom until we adequately identify and address the things that are keeping us bound. Joining your voice with the witness of others' experiences only strengthens your voice. It's hard to silence someone who has a story to tell, and it's even harder to silence a group of people who are all telling the same story.

Naming our own constellation of harms isn't about having a so-called "victim mentality." Telling people that they have a victim mentality is a silencing tactic that shames them into accepting adverse circumstances. All this does is serve the people and institutions perpetuating injustice, and it places an undue burden of shame on people who just want their lives to be different.

Implicit in the claim of a victim mentality is the assumption that people don't want to take responsibility for their actions. While it's true that some people will blame-shift when they're caught making a bad choice, an individual seeking to shift blame for a situation for which they bare sole responsibility is different from people naming and seeking to right wrongs that are committed against them.

Recognizing our constellation of harms shouldn't push us into blame-shifting by making our bad decisions someone else's responsibility, nor should it cause us to despair when everything seems out of our control. Recognizing our constellation of harms gives us the gift of self-determination—the ability for a person to make decisions for themselves. We might not be able to control our circumstances, but we can let our experiences empower us to recognize our part in making our world better and free us to push back against injustice.

What constellation of harms has led you to this point in your justice-seeking journey? Who or what has tried to silence you over the years? How will you use those experiences to free yourself and to seek justice now?

3

LOSING MY VOICE

White Kids Say the Darndest Things

In the aftermath of Grandma's cancer diagnosis, I often felt like I couldn't do anything right. I was always getting in trouble for talking back to adults, and my family's patience with my verbosity seemed to be wearing thin. But Mrs. Donaldson's fifth-grade class was the one place in the world where I felt I could do no wrong. While the entropy of injustice threatened to hurl me into a black hole, in Mrs. Donaldson's class, I felt like a supernova giving off its brightest light before being sucked into the abyss. Mrs. Donaldson treated me like a star that was among the biggest and brightest in the galaxy of her classroom. I was at the peak of self-confidence then; I believed that I could do or be absolutely anything in the world. Everywhere else, I was too tall, too loud, too opinionated, and way too much, but Mrs. Donaldson made me feel as if there was always enough room for all of me.

I had big ideas, a big personality, and a big voice to match. At five feet, five inches tall, I was three inches away from my adult height, making me the tallest kid in my class, the second-tallest kid in my grade, and the tallest girl by a mile. I looked like an adult compared to my peers.

I regularly got the top score on tests in every subject, but I excelled in history. I eagerly raised my hand to answer questions and to share the historical facts that I knew, and Mrs. Donaldson was eager to call on me. I had memorized all of the presidents in order in second grade, and I could easily rattle off some of their terms in office. I knew an interesting fact or two about their personal lives and presidencies, and I could also name many of the vice presidents. Since the fifth-grade curriculum emphasized American history, my years of independent study on the topic made me excited to finally put my knowledge to use in the classroom.

For a long time, I had a reputation among my peers of being one of the smartest—if not *the* smartest—person in our grade. (My senior superlative was Most Scholarly Girl. I would go on to marry the Most Scholarly Boy, who was also the valedictorian of our class.) For most of elementary school, my intellectual acumen earned me a place of respect among my peers.

However, something changed in fifth grade. I was usually among the leaders and deciders of what was "cool" in my classroom, but that year I was put in the same room as some of the most popular kids in my grade who were also used to being the tastemakers in their respective classrooms.

Suddenly, I had to compete for the attention and positive regard of my classmates. In years past, my classmates had almost universally found my jokes funny (or so I thought), they had been impressed with my knowledge (or so I thought), and they thought that I was cool (or so I thought). Now, there was a group of kids who did everything they could to let me know that I wasn't funny, wasn't cool, and that my intellectualism was something that annoyed them. On the outside, I played it cool. I kept up with my jokes, kept raising my hand in class, and kept up the facade that I was the coolest kid in Mrs. Donaldson's class. Internally, I schemed and plotted about what I could do to get them to like me. One day, opportunity knocked.

Although I lived close enough to walk to school, my mom worked in Kansas City so I had to get up early and ride the school bus from Grandma's house on the other side of town. When the bus dropped me off, I would go to the school gym to wait until it was time for class. We called this the "bus room," and it was the epicenter of elementary school wheeling, dealing, and social climbing.

In the bus room, each grade sat on the floor in a section of the gym. We were supposed to sit in a line, but the lines always devolved into linear camps stretching the width of the basketball court. Since the bus room was sorted by grade and not by classroom, it was the perfect place to connect with friends who were in other classes or to make new friends. In the bus room, it seemed, the boundaries of friendships and cliques were blurred, and one could make friends and be friends with virtually anyone.

On most days, I sat in line with Sadie, one of my closest friends. We weren't in the same classroom that year, but we were in the same reading and math classes. Sadie was a social butterfly and could get along with just about anybody. She was levelheaded and a meticulous rule follower. I was adventurous and had no problem challenging the rules or social norms if it ultimately led to something good. I would often talk her into joining me in my latest harebrained scheme or flight of fancy, and she would reluctantly go along with it as long as I promised that we wouldn't get in trouble or embarrass ourselves.

Somehow or another, I had gotten it into my mind that the way to maintain my "cool" status was to sit near a group of the popular boys in our grade in the bus room, and so I enlisted Sadie to join me in my latest endeavor. She was the only one of my girl friends who wasn't afraid to be around boys so she was the perfect sidekick.

We started off just sitting near them, Sadie's easygoing manner and charm winning them over and my subject matter expertise grabbing—if not maintaining—their attention. I was a tomboy and leveraged my tomboyishness to engage with them and try to show them just how cool I was. I made jokes, told stories, and tried to wow them. Sadie was there to keep the conversation going and make sure I had at least one person listening to my schtick.

Things were going great (or so I thought).

"You talk too much," one of the boys, Milton, said one Monday morning. He seemed angry, though I didn't know why. I didn't feel like I had been saying any more than anyone else in the group. In fact, when I did speak, they frequently talked over me or ignored what I said.

"No I don't," I retorted, feeling indignant. I started to feel self-conscious, and so I quickly attempted to hide my insecurity.

"Yes you do," Milton responded. "I bet you couldn't go the whole week without talking."

"How much do you wanna bet that I could?" I snapped back.

Suddenly, the group of kids who was only ever half interested in anything I said or did gave me their full attention.

"You couldn't go a whole week without talking. You wouldn't even make it through the rest of the day," Milton said.

Some of the other boys started to chime in. Their responses were a mix of mocking, scorn, and playfulness. I couldn't tell if they were laughing with me or at me. I chose to believe that they were my friends who were giving me a hard time about something, though I was confused by the sudden turn in the conversation and why some of them seemed so mad.

"How much do you wanna bet?" I repeated.

"I'm not paying you any money," Milton replied. "But I know you would lose."

"I would not." I was starting to get angry. If there's anything in the world that gets me going, it's somebody telling me that I can't do something.

"So then take the bet," he said.

I shoved my hand in Milton's direction so we could shake on it. I shook hands with the other boys in the group and shut my mouth. Milton wasn't in Mrs. Donaldson's class, but a couple of the other boys were, so they were deputized to make sure I didn't speak.

I didn't know what I would get if I won the bet, and I didn't know what I would have to do if I lost, but I didn't care. I had never backed down from a dare, and I wasn't about to start. Those boys had told me that I couldn't do something, and I was determined to show them that I could.

Just as the bet was sealed, we were dismissed from the bus room. I marched from the gym with a small entourage of fifth graders surrounding me, trying any and every trick in the book to get me to talk, but I remained silent as a tomb. Sadie stood beside me, amazed that I had taken the bet and probably a bit bewildered that I wasn't speaking. We had been friends since second grade, and this was the quietest she had ever seen me.

I walked into Mrs. Donaldson's classroom with my head held high and my mouth closed. She must have sensed that something was amiss as half the class stared at me and the other half tried to figure out what the commotion was about.

"What's going on?" she asked, looking to me for an explanation.

I stared back at her, my face stoic, my lips sealed. Giggles erupted from those who were in the know.

"Are you okay?" Mrs. Donaldson asked, concerned.

I nodded.

"She made a bet that she could go the whole week without talking," Felix, one of Milton's emissaries, spoke up.

I smiled and nodded.

Mrs. Donaldson looked uneasy. "Who was the bet with?"

Felix listed off the names of the boys involved. Most of them were in her reading class.

Mrs. Donaldson looked back at me, and I smiled at her. She seemed a bit troubled, and I wondered if I had done something wrong. It was too late though. The bet had been made, and I was determined not to go back on my word.

We began our first subject, and when Mrs. Donaldson asked the first question of the day, everyone looked in my direction. I lifted my chin defiantly, my hands folded on top of my desk, and stared back at everyone. Someone else answered the question and class went on.

I resumed my defiant pose as we traded classrooms for reading. Mrs. Donaldson was also my reading teacher, so I remained at my desk and smiled as Sadie, Milton, and most of the other boys who were involved with the bet filed into the room. Felix updated them on my progress. Of course, I hadn't talked.

I continued my silence through reading class, even as Mrs. Donaldson kept looking at me, her face etched with concern. I could tell that she didn't like the bet, and I felt conflicted because I didn't want to do anything that would lower my stock with her. Later that day, she pulled me aside and told me that I was a good student and she depended on my participation to help her. I don't know how true it was, but hearing her say that made me feel like a million dollars. No one in my life had ever invited me to talk more, let alone told me that they needed me to talk.

The week went on and I continued to stay quiet, except when it was time to participate in class. Soon, my classmates started to realize how inconvenient my silence was for them, and they would give me "permission" to answer their questions or give my opinion about something. Even with participating in class and answering the occasional question, I was still quiet and rationed my participation and engagement with others.

I was dead set on proving that I was capable of being quiet. If people thought I talked too much, then I was going to show them

I didn't have to talk at all. If being quiet meant people wouldn't be angry with me, then so be it. If shutting up meant I would have friends and people would think I was cool, then losing my voice was a small price to pay.

That Friday, I left Mrs. Donaldson's room feeling as if I had climbed Mount Everest. The following Monday, I made my triumphant return to the bus room.

"I won the bet," I shouted, taking my seat among the losers.

Milton sat, unmoved.

"OK, so what do I get?" I asked.

"Nothing," he said.

"Nothing? But I was quiet the whole week!"

"Well, I hoped that you would never talk anywhere ever again. You're so annoying," Milton snapped.

I was hurt, but I wasn't about to let him see it. "Yeah, well you're annoying too," I jeered.

"Shut up, jigaboo."

A couple of the other boys laughed.

I had no idea what a jigaboo was.

"You shut up, dork," I retorted.

"Spear thrower," Milton responded unfazed. More chuckles from others around us.

I had no idea what a spear thrower was and didn't understand why it would be an insult, but there was something about how he said it that let me know it was more than a run-of-the-mill diss.

"Butt munch," I snarled, angry that Milton was laughing at his own silly jabs while acting totally unaffected by mine.

"Leave me alone, porch monkey," he said with a laugh.

My heart skipped a beat. I knew what a porch monkey was.

A feeling of ugliness and shame washed over me as I tried to catch my breath. Although I had never heard the other slurs before,

I instantly surmised that they were intended to have the same effect. I was shocked that Milton knew so many awful names for Black people, and it immediately and forever changed my opinion of him. He knew exactly what he was saying to me, and it was clear that he intended to demean me in front of everyone.

Milton sardonically laughed as I shrank back, his cruelty rendering me speechless. I knew that telling a teacher would be about as useful as trying to build a house with a glass hammer; I had been called the n-word at least twice before at school, and the perpetrators never got more than a "now, now" before they were sent on their racist way. If the teachers didn't know how to act when somebody called me a whole nigger, I knew they wouldn't know what to do with jigaboo, spear thrower, and porch monkey.

Milton and the other boys turned their backs to me, and I sat in the bus line feeling angry and humiliated. When Sadie finally arrived, I didn't tell her what had happened. I was too hurt and embarrassed, and it felt awkward to share something so disgraceful with a white person, even if she was one of my closest friends.

What I experienced in the bus room that morning was misogynoir wearing braces and a bowl cut. Misogynoir is a term that was coined by Moya Bailey, a Black feminist scholar, to describe the racialized sexism that Black women experience.[1] It perfectly describes Milton's behavior. He wasn't annoyed that I talked too much. What bothered him was that I had the audacity to show up in the world the way that I did—as a loud Black girl. When he realized he couldn't shut me up with the bet, he decided he would shut me up some other way.

1. moyazb [Moya Bailey], "They aren't talking about me…," *Crunk Feminist Collective* (blog), March 14, 2010, https://www.crunkfeministcollective.com/2010/03/14/they-arent-talking-about-me/.

Somewhere along the line, Milton learned the way to shut a Black person up was to call them hateful names, and not just any hateful names—he chose racial epithets that have a long and hurtful history behind them. It's wild that an eleven-year-old realized he held that kind of power over another person. The sophistication with which he wielded those words showed a level of precision and specificity that isn't gained by mindlessly repeating something he heard somebody else say; it comes with study and practice. It's the difference between identifying a color as green, yellow-green, or chartreuse. There's levels to it. You don't pick that junk up from the racist uncle you only see once a year.

Milton wasn't the first little white boy to talk slick to me, and he was nowhere near the last. As an adult, I have experienced similar emotional outbursts from grown white men who were angry that I wasn't reflexively deferential and subservient to them. Milton was the prepubescent version of every white man who has ever tried to shut me up. They might not all have played vicious jokes or used racial slurs, but they have all been angry about how I choose to use my voice.

I felt foolish for not realizing the bet was a cruel joke intended to shame me. Milton's outburst showed me there was also a racial component to how he and the other boys had treated me. There I was, one of only a handful of Black kids in fifth grade, allowing a group of white kids to determine whether and how much I got to speak. When I realized how I must have looked, it made me sick to my stomach. My family had always impressed upon me the importance of representing Black people well when I was around white folks, and they taught me that I shouldn't do anything that was demeaning or played into negative stereotypes. When I realized that I had "put on a show" and behaved in a way that had garnered white attention for all the wrong reasons, I felt like I had let all the other Black kids down. I would feel this sting many more times as I learned to navigate living under the white gaze.

I was no stranger to overt racism; I had experienced at least one overtly racist incident (and countless microaggressions) nearly every year of elementary school. What got me about the incident with Milton was the abruptness with which it happened and the suddenness with which it all seemed to be forgotten—two factors that have been present in almost every racist incident that I've ever experienced. What nobody tells you is that racism will run up on you, sucker punch you in the chest, then walk off like it ain't no thang. Or at least that's how racism is set up in small, predominantly white towns. People will pop off with some of the most ignorant, hurtful, and racist crap and then go on about their day like nothing happened. Some of them will even have the temerity to laugh about it as they keep on keepin' on. Outside of someone having a reputation for being racist, there's no way to know for sure who will pop off next or what will set them off. Everything will be high fives and cool vibes until you cross some invisible line and then it's anger and racial slurs.

Experience had taught me that it wasn't a matter of *if* some white kid would decide to say something racist to me, but *when*. The incident in the bus room reinforced to me that I was never truly safe from experiencing racism. It didn't matter how smart, funny, or popular I was, racism would always be the noose hung round my neck. With one false move, any white person could leave me hanging like strange fruit. And they wouldn't even be punished for it, which left me feeling absolutely powerless.

As I sat in the bus room trying to pretend that everything was fine, I realized that everything wasn't fine. In that moment, I lost my voice.

With only a few exceptions, every Black person I know who has spent any kind of time in white-dominated spaces has had some version of what I call The Moment—a point in time when a white person shows their whole racist self and we are reminded (or learn for the first time) that people will abuse, despise, and revile us for simply existing in melanated skin. Most of the time, these realizations come to us in our formative years, as children and teenagers, but there are also full-grown adults (often those who were sheltered from racial realities in their upbringing) who come by this knowledge later in life.

Some people describe The Moment as the first time they were called a slur or experienced other racist, demeaning speech and actions. Others describe The Moment as incidents of exclusion or disparate treatment. For some people, The Moment shows up as broken trust when close friends and associates let their racism slip out and then rush to reassure us we are not like *other* Black folks and so we shouldn't be offended. Sometimes The Moment comes as the sudden recognition of the lies we have believed about ourselves (or other Black folk) and that no matter how much we try to adapt and assimilate to whiteness we will never be white and will always be treated accordingly. However The Moment shows up, it is guaranteed to be perplexing and hurtful.

Being Black in white space means living and reliving different iterations of The Moment like a recurring sleep paralysis nightmare. The Moment strikes like a thief in the night, catching us unawares and looting our dignity and sense of well-being. Even when we have defenses in place, The Moment can still leave us feeling shaken and disoriented as we try to make sense of what happened.

The Moment threatens to force us into silence—not just in The Moment but forever.

White people's rage at having their racism brought to their attention in The Moment is oftentimes more dangerous than The Moment itself. We learn to adhere to their code of silence about race (at least in their presence) out of self-preservation so that we don't experience the fullness of white rage. We learn to shut up so that we won't be shut up.

In the bus room that day, the message that it wasn't safe to be loud and Black was reinforced, yet again, to fifth-grade me. In the years to come, my various talents would continue to place me in others' high esteem. As I experienced increasing favor, I learned that the praise I received from white people came with the tacit agreement that I would not upset their status quo. Whatever un-seasoned swill white dominance dished out, I was expected to take with a smile on my face and gratitude on my lips. The juxtaposition of white praise and white rage became a diamond-encrusted muzzle that would stifle my voice for years. In time, I would cast my fears aside and remove the muzzle, but the road to freedom was stony and the punishment for failing to conform bitter. For years, I was afraid to speak up when I experienced racism.

Losing your voice can be a frustrating, hurtful experience. You don't have to remain silent though. You can take off the muzzle. In the words of Assata Shakur, "[You] have nothing to lose but [your] chains."[2]

2. Assata Shakur, Angela Y. Davis, and Lennox S. Hinds, *Assata: An Autobiography* (Chicago: Lawrence Hill, 1987), 52.

4

UNPRETTY (I WANNA DANCE WITH SOMEBODY)

When You Fail the Beauty Standard
and the Beauty Standard Fails You

Attending the back-to-school dance at the civic center was a rite of passage for the teenagers in my little town. The back-to-school dance was different from the dances held on school grounds because it was chaperoned by a group of local volunteers who were (at least in our perception) slightly more permissive than teachers. It was also the first dance of the year, which made it the social event of the season. My first dance was in sixth grade during the final days of summer in 1997. I was ecstatic for the dance and secretly hoped that a cute boy would notice me and ask me to dance and that we would sway back and forth to "Truly, Madly, Deeply" by Savage Garden while longingly gazing into one another's eyes. Then maybe, just maybe, he would ask me to be his girlfriend.

That night, I decided to wear a brown button-down polyester shirt that had black and white squares on it with a pair of black hip-hugger bell-bottoms and chunky, black platform shoes. My mom bumped the ends of my Toni Braxton haircut, and you couldn't tell me nothing when I stepped out the car and strutted into that civic center, honey.

As I made my way onto the dance floor, I searched the cavernous gymnasium for a familiar face, any familiar face. I was relieved to find Monique, my best friend, and we quickly gathered a group of friends and started dancing.

By Black standards, I'm not much of a dancer, but in rural Missouri all a Black girl needs is confidence and a modicum of rhythm and folks will think you are Janet Jackson. Thankfully, Monique was a legitimately good dancer and so I didn't have to shoulder the burden of teaching the Rhythmless Nation (aka the crowd of sixth-grade girls gathered around us who acted like they never danced in public before) how to stay on beat during "The Macarena." Monique was cute and effortlessly cool, and dancing with her made me feel cute and effortlessly cool too. The other advantage to dancing with Monique was that she was biracial, and so she could code-switch her dancing style based on the song, which was very helpful when "Tubthumping" by Chumbawumba came on because I had no idea how to dance to that.

We were dancing the night away when it happened. The familiar strains of "Always Be My Baby" blared from the large speakers on the gymnasium stage indicating the first slow dance of the night. Our girl power dance group broke up quicker than the Spice Girls as everyone started pairing off. I looked around, waiting for someone to ask me. The seventh and eighth grade couples were already swaying together, and I quickly lost hope of being asked to dance by an older boy. As my fellow sixth graders awkwardly sought and found dance partners, I realized that nobody was going to ask me to dance.

I decided to take matters into my own hands and started asking boys if they wanted to dance with me. Some of them politely declined my offer. Others said that maybe they would another time. But for every polite no or maybe, there was another boy who was condescending or outright mean in his refusal. The number of boys who were angry or disgusted by the thought of dancing with me left me feeling hurt and devastated. Being given a curt no isn't what hurt my feelings. It was the grossed-out looks and the how-dare-you attitudes that stung, especially when they came from boys who I was otherwise friendly with. I couldn't understand why so many boys would rather wait in line for another girl than dance with me, who was willing and available.

The song faded out and everyone returned to their friend groups to gossip and giggle about who they danced with. My disappointment hung like a millstone around my neck. I put on a fake smile and tried to act happy for my friends who had gotten to dance with their crushes or who found a new crush during the slow dance.

As the evening wore on, I found myself in a feedback loop of hope and hurt. As I danced with my girl friends, I hoped that someone would be mustering up the courage to ask me to dance. Then, as the next slow dance started, my hope would bleed into hurt as I desperately tried to find someone, anyone, to dance with. I watched boys who had acted grossed out at the prospect of dancing with me smile as their hands gingerly slipped around another girl's waist. The boys who said they would dance with me on another song offered the same excuse again, and the ones who had politely declined became annoyed when I circled back. The song faded and I was left standing alone again. Lather, rinse, repeat.

At the end of the night, I sullenly slunk into the back seat of my mom's car.

"Did you have a good time?" she asked.

"Yeah," I lied as I groped for my seat belt in the dark. I didn't feel like sharing my dashed romantic hopes with my mom.

"Did you dance with anyone?"

Of course she had to ask that.

"No. None of the boys wanted to dance with me," I replied, hoping that she would drop the subject.

"Not even Marcus or De'Andre?"

Clearly, Mom didn't understand what the word *none* meant.

"They had a ton of girls who were trying to dance with them all night." I sighed. Marcus and De'Andre were the only two Black boys in my grade, and they were my play cousins. It would've been extremely awkward to put too much energy into trying to dance with either of them.

Mom started to list different boys in my grade, wondering if I had asked them. I interrupted her, now in full twelve-year-old meltdown mode. "NOBODY wanted to dance with me. I asked every boy in the sixth grade if they wanted to dance. They were either dancing with somebody else, didn't want to dance, or didn't want to dance with me. EVERYBODY else got to dance with somebody, but I didn't."

"Well, there's always the next dance," Mom replied.

I sighed and pretended to look out the window so I could get away with rolling my eyes.

Things didn't get better at the next dance or even the dance after that. Throughout middle school, songs like "All My Life," "I Don't Want to Miss a Thing," and "I'll Be" served as the soundtrack for being repeatedly rejected by the boys in my grade and a few of the older boys who I knew too. There were at least three different dances every year, and so I experienced a lot of rejection. In seventh grade, I started to accept that just about all of the boys who enjoyed slow dancing would never choose me as their partner. Occasionally, I could convince one of my guy friends to dance for one song, but I learned that I would never be anyone's first choice. The best I could do was take a pity lap during the bridge of "My Heart Will Go On" when one of my guy friends didn't get the partner he wanted.

The issue wasn't that the boys didn't want to dance with me—they had the right to turn me down if they didn't want to dance—it was the way that I was rejected. In my mind's eye, I could see the scowls and looks of revulsion on some of my classmates' faces when I asked them to dance, and this communicated disdain at the idea of dancing *with me*. The way that I was rejected let me know that there was something about me that was undesirable, something that didn't change from dance to dance or from sixth to seventh grade. I vacillated between self-pity, envy, anger, frustration, longing, and melancholy: an emotional cocktail that left me hung over with confusion and vexed with myself for caring so freaking much.

The sound of broken promises to dance on the next slow song would fill my ears, and I wondered why I fell for it every time. The sting of rejection pummeled me like angry waves crashing against the shoreline, each billow eroding my confidence and self-worth.

At first, I didn't have language for how I felt. Then, in the summer before eighth grade, Aunties T-Boz, Left Eye, and Chilli gave me the word that I needed to describe my experiences: Unpretty. That was it. I felt Unpretty.

Feeling Unpretty has little to do with how you actually look; it is about how not fitting society's beauty standards makes you feel on the inside and how you choose to respond to it. I knew that I could *never* fit the beauty standard that was prevalent among my peers in my small town, let alone the standards that were being foisted on me by MTV and the various teen magazines that were a staple of my media consumption. The clothes, makeup, and hairstyles of the day didn't look the same on me. My skin was too dark, my hair too nappy, my nose too broad, my lips too thick. Furthermore, I didn't *want* to fit the beauty standard; I wanted the people around me to recognize the beauty that God gave me.

There has not been a single day in my life where I wished that I was white. For me, desiring whiteness would have been the same as denying the struggles of those who came before me, as well as my own lived experience. I wouldn't dare disrespect my Elders, Ancestors, or myself like that. Until I read *The Bluest Eye* when

I was fifteen, it never even occurred to me that any Black person could earnestly want to be anything other than Black. Yet, my spirit was steadily being crushed under the weight of feeling Unpretty because the very things that make me who I am—the things that make me Black—were constantly treated as abnormal and insignificant.

Beauty culture tells women that our value lies in our ability to attract and retain male attention, and our ability to attract and retain male attention is almost exclusively based on our physical appearance. For all the gains the women's movement has made over the past two centuries, we have done little to escape from a beauty culture that elevates white, able-bodied, cisgender, heterosexual, skinny bodies over and above everyone else. It's hard to take these so-called advancements seriously when the overall culture remains the same. Photo spreads that include fat women, disabled women, or women wearing hijab ring hollow when they are treated as an attempt to meet a quota instead of an opportunity to change the status quo. The only thing worse than outright exclusion is condescending inclusion that values our presence as long as we agree that we won't do too much to confront our oppression.

In beauty culture, people who hold contested identities are treated not as equals with the ability to redefine or destroy beauty standards, but as "influences" or "inspiration" for white women's journeys to self-actualization, if their "influence" or "inspiration" is acknowledged at all. Marginalized folks are seen as second-class women, if they're considered women at all. Until beauty culture ascribes value to them, they are nothing. They are nonbeing. They are Unpretty.

Overlapping the Eurocentric (that is, white-dominated) beauty culture are the beauty cultures created by people of the global majority. It is important to note that these beauty cultures exist *alongside* and *overlap* the Eurocentric beauty culture; they are not subcultures. People of the global majority had their own ideas of beauty that existed long before the proliferation of white supremacy into global society.

In the United States, people of color's beauty standards have shifted to simultaneously oppose and adapt to white supremacy. In other words, people of the global majority have their own beauty cultures that started as an expression of their cultural identities before encountering white people, but white supremacy has caused them to adapt to the Eurocentric beauty standard in some ways, while rejecting Eurocentrism in others. For example, someone might wear a wig with straight hair to fit in with the environment of their workplace but wear their natural hair on the weekends. Wearing a wig isn't inherently Eurocentric, but wearing a wig to work might be an adaptation that a Black person makes to avoid being penalized for looking "unprofessional" or being dehumanized by people touching their natural hair.

Even as people of color engage with our own beauty cultures, white supremacy can prevent us from rightly seeing ourselves and one another. Eurocentrism ensures the exploitation of bodies that are closer to the Eurocentric beauty standard and the marginalization of everyone else. Lateral oppression (the prejudice and harm that racially minoritized groups commit against one another) ensures that people of the global majority will do harm to one another as they vie for validation under the white beauty standard. Anti-Blackness ensures that Black people (especially dark-skinned Black people) are consistently pushed to the bottom of the racial beauty hierarchy.

Additionally, many of us grew up with messages from our own communities that reinforced beauty standards that are steeped in white supremacy. We were told that our skin was too dark, or that our lips were too big, or that our hair texture was inferior, or that our bodies were otherwise unacceptable. Some of us carried these messages with us into adulthood and continue to allow them to shape our self-image and how we allow our bodies to show up in the world. What would happen if we dropped our defenses, our objections, and our well-thought-out reasons for conforming to the dominant beauty standard? What if we did the difficult work of examining why we believe certain negative things about our bodies? What would happen if we examined our own assumptions about what is beautiful and chose to embrace a standard of beauty that liberates rather than oppresses?

Meanwhile, white people—who obliterated their own ethnicities and sense of culture in service to white supremacy—are perfectly comfortable with stealing from us the same beauty that they told us we couldn't have. While we are out here policing one another's beauty, they are steady robbing us and repackaging our beauty as their own. White supremacy tells us that our bodies are unacceptable and so they must be filtered through whiteness in order to be considered beautiful. The message is clear: Whiteness is beautiful. We are Unpretty.

As a teenager, I was acutely aware of society's beauty standards. I felt their impact on my Black body, but I felt powerless to do or say anything about it. I realize that feeling Unpretty is a common experience for young people, especially during those tumultuous years of puberty where our bodies are changing and our brains are still developing. A lot of us look back with a sense of horror over the clothes we used to wear, the people we used to have crushes on, and the social rejection and isolation we felt back then. A lot of us have scars from that time that run deep into our souls, whether they be from bullying, rejection, self-hatred, or a myriad of other misfortunes and injustices.

For me, the issue extended far beyond not getting a dance partner. I recognized that my peers likely had their own reasons for not wanting to dance with me and that some of those reasons might not have had anything to do with my race. But when folks consistently turn their nose up at the idea of dancing with you, at talking on the phone with you, at going on a date with you, at being your boyfriend, or at doing basic crap like treating you as if you are a human being, you can't help but wonder if something more sinister is afoot.

White supremacy tells us that no matter what we do, we will always be Unpretty, and so we should shut up and accept our lot. It tells us that wearing our hair the way that it grows out of our head is too loud, and so we have to shut up and wear more "professional" hairstyles or fight to change policies and pass demeaning laws that give us permission to exist. White supremacy tells us that our big earrings and bright lipstick are too loud, and so we have to shut up and take out our earrings and wipe off our makeup so we can be taken seriously. It tells us that, regardless of our size or shape, our bodies take up too much space, and so we must shut up and make ourselves smaller so we can fit into the tiny boxes they try to shove us into.

The good news is that we don't have to shut up. We don't have to accept the lie that we are Unpretty. We don't have to keep tamping ourselves down and shoving ourselves into boxes that were not created for our flourishing. We can embrace the fullness of our identities and walk in healing. But we can't be healed until we can take an honest look inside and examine the lies that we believe about ourselves and our Blackness. When we become fully healed, we can be truly free. Freedom don't come easy. We can't be free if we are still tightly clinging to the bosom of white supremacy. But when we do the risky and difficult work of detaching ourselves from white supremacist frameworks, we give ourselves something greater: freedom. Oh freedom!

5

WHITE NOISE

When White Supremacy Seems Totally Normal

White noise—also known as static—is an even hissing or shushing sound, similar to the noise that an air conditioner makes or the blowing sound of a box fan. It is a random sequence of every frequency that is possible for humans to hear played at the same decibel level. It has the ability to mask other sounds, which is why white noise machines are a popular choice among people who need to minimize distractions for study or sleep. White noise easily fades into the background and becomes part of the ambiance of almost any room. Our senses effortlessly adapt to it; we may not even realize that white noise is playing unless it suddenly becomes too loud.

When white noise is played loudly, it has a harsh, grating sound. This type of static is familiar to anyone who grew up listening to the radio or seeing the black-and-white "snow" on television before digital tuners were invented. Static let you know to change the channel because there was nothing to see or hear. Little can compare to the shock that came with accidentally pressing the wrong combination of numbers on the television remote and being accosted by static blaring through the speakers.

White noise can be either a soothing shush that placates our senses or a harsh static that leaves us flailing to make an adjustment when we push the wrong buttons.

White noise is also the steady drone of white supremacy that follows us practically everywhere we go. Its frequencies contain the range of human experience, except that those experiences are corrupted by racism. It is the everyday racism that we accept as such a part of living that we often don't even recognize it as oppression. We sometimes find ourselves acquiescing to the white noise of subtle racism lest we do something to trigger a loud, offensive blast of racist static from white people.

White noise is The Racist Way That Things Are. It is the overarching presence and compounding effects of racism. It's the subtle shush of white supremacy that can lull us into accepting oppression as normative. It is a whiteness-dominated culture that rewards assimilation and oppresses anyone who doesn't or can't code-switch. It's an environment in which speaking against racism causes far more offense than people being racist. It's the myriad injustices and inequities that we observe on a regular basis. It's all the so-called microaggressions, the small, seemingly insignificant things—like your body always being poorly lit in group pictures, or people cutting in front of you in line, or having to do your own makeup for the school play, or having to pay extra to get the Black channels on cable—the "little things" that compound into a constellation of harms over time. Every so often, white noise becomes the harsh static of overt racism that leaves us flailing as we attempt to hit the mute button and change the channel to a less racist station.

White noise isn't one thing. It is everything. It is in everything. And until you learn otherwise, it seems completely normal. White noise is always there, steadily providing a racist backdrop to the most mundane activities. At its absolute best, white noise is an inevitable annoyance that comes with navigating a world that makes it easy for white people to act racist. It's something we put up with because we know things could always be much worse. At its absolute worst, white noise becomes such a part of our environment that we fail to perceive it, and challenging it becomes tantamount to challenging our own sense of value or place in the world. Racism can become so normalized that we will try to explain it away or get defensive when people try to tell us that we don't have to live this way.

White noise conditions us to accept the status quo. It teaches us to "go along to get along" because it is much easier to tolerate something that feels relatively insignificant than to deal with the inevitable white rage that comes with telling someone they are being racist. White noise teaches us that there are consequences if we speak too loudly about injustice. It teaches us to swallow injustice and indignity because the threat of even worse treatment looms around the corner if we speak out. We learn to make little adjustments and accommodations that seem insignificant at the time but eventually add up. "Going along to get along" buys us the absence of conflict, but the cost is our freedom.

Growing up Black in a predominantly white town meant that I was surrounded by the white noise of racism. There isn't a singular scenario or incident I can point to that will adequately illustrate the prevalence of white noise in this setting. It's not a matter of one racist thing happening multiple times or multiple racist things happening once; it's living under the constant threat that some-body's ignorance can hurt, harm, or kill you. It's bracing yourself for someone to call you a racial slur when they get upset with you. It's finding out that your crush likes you too, but they can't go out with you because their family wouldn't approve. It's people feeling entitled to ask you ignorant and inappropriate questions about your body. It's the humiliation you feel when people try to discreetly wipe their hands after touching you.

This isn't to say that my upbringing was all bad or that I didn't have any meaningful, life-giving interactions with the white people back home. I have many lifelong friendships with white school-mates that still bring me joy. The most enduring relationship I have with a white person from my hometown is with my husband, Ben, whom I met in band during our freshman year of high school. I have at least as many fond recollections of small-town life as I do negative memories. Yet, within even the most pleasant of remem-brances is the faint shush of white noise.

By the time I entered high school, I learned to expect and accept racism from white people. I learned that a lot of white folks had no compunction about being racist, and so I thought that it was my job to try to mitigate or avoid their racism altogether. A morbid, self-deprecating sense of humor became my defense mechanism against what I had accepted as inevitable. Instead of being the butt of racist jokes, I found that I could reclaim my power by saying what I thought people were already thinking. The jokes don't hurt as much as when you make them about yourself.

Being a superminority—the term I use to describe anyone who lives in a context that is greater than 80 percent white—means learning to be judicious about giving pushback when you experi-ence racism. Most of the time, it costs way more to push back against white noise than it does to acquiesce to it. You become willing to shoulder "lighter" oppression for the sake of "keeping the peace" because if you speak up about racism too much, people (even the few other Black folks in your context) will call you "loud" and accuse you of "stirring the pot" and being a "troublemaker"— I know because people have said these things about me.

As a superminority I learned that managing white people's racism was my responsibility. I learned not to do anything that would make white people angry with me and thus incite their racism. I learned not to invite white people's racism by doing anything that could play into stereotypes about Black people. I learned that it was my job to prevent white people from acting on their worst impulses.

Growing up as a superminority taught me that racism is such a part of white culture that they don't even consider their behavior to be racist. To be sure, white people know what racism is, but white individuals fool themselves into believing they and most of the white people they know aren't racist. They convince themselves that their behavior is perfectly acceptable, and they are more than willing to tell each other that their behavior is acceptable so they don't have to own up to the truth. Then they try to gaslight us into believing that if we call them on their racism, we are the problem.

When you repeatedly receive messages that communicate that your pain is insignificant, you eventually learn to shut up about it. What good does it do to say that something hurts when people ignore you or try to convince you that your pain isn't real?

Being a superminority taught me to be silent about oppression.

When oppression threatens to silence you, you have a choice to make: push back or shut up.

Shutting up seems like a viable option until you realize what it costs. When you are silent about your subjugation, it doesn't stop people from subjugating you. If anything, it gives them permission to keep that same energy and to treat you as if you asked to be mistreated. When you push back against oppression, you might pay for it in lost opportunities, broken relationships, and other types of immediate, temporal consequences. What you gain, however, is the ability to maintain your dignity.

Many years ago, I asked my grandma what the word *dignity* meant. She answered by singing some old song that said, "I've got my dignity to keep me warm." I don't know if it was an actual song or something she made up, but that song has stayed with me all these years. Whenever I hear the word *dignity*, I automatically think of this song and how true it is.

When you push back against oppression, you might experience other painful losses, but at least you can keep your self-respect.

By the time I went off to college, I had started to believe that racism was an inevitable part of life that I was absolutely powerless to change. I thought it was my job to prevent white people from being racist against me. I believed that if I could show them that I was a "good" Black person then maybe, just maybe, I wouldn't experience racism. Oh, how I wish I had known back then that I could push back against racism! It would have saved me so much unnecessary hurt and shame. But I didn't know what I didn't know, and so I had to learn this important life lesson the hard way.

EASY ON ME

Why I Chose to Write into the Wound

As I write this intermission, Adele's song "Easy On Me" is #4 on the *Billboard* Hot 100 chart. ("We Don't Talk About Bruno" from Disney's *Encanto* is #1; that song is my *jam*.) A song about going easy on yourself for the decisions and failings of your youth seemed like an apt title for this part of my story. I hope that I am able to go easy on myself as I write about the hard-won knowledge that came from being in a bunch of unpleasant situations.

I hope that I am able to go easy on myself because it is actually pretty humiliating to talk about the racist stuff I experienced as a young adult. I blame myself for allowing my inexperience and naivety to keep me in a bunch of janky situations instead of getting out. Accepting racism as an inevitable part of life taught me to cater to white people's comfort in order to survive. I was afraid that if I spoke out too loudly, I would lose opportunities, friendships, and my place in the world.

In Act II, you will see me stay in several situations that I clearly should have left. You also will see me return to people and places that were harmful to me. If you are reading and think, *Girl, why didn't you just let them people alone*, know that I have asked myself that question about a hundred thousand times. The utterly unsatisfying answer in many cases is that I struggled to recognize when people were doing me wrong, and I believed I was powerless to stop white people from being racist—until I found my voice and gained the courage to stand up for myself. I will try to say why I made certain choices when we get there, but the thing to bear in mind is that toxic people will have you convinced that *you* are the problem. And so I attached myself to toxic people and situations because I was not yet free enough to recognize that *I* was not the problem.

I feel angry that, for so long, I thought it was my responsibility to silently endure racism rather than to push back. I thought justice seeking required me to remain in contested space as some kind of good faith gesture, and so I desired unity with people who were more invested in their comfort than in fighting injustice. There are so many times that I wish I could hop in a time machine and go back and tell people that they were doing me wrong. I wish I could go back and stand up for myself while boldly calling out the nonsense. No such apparatus exists, and so I must live with the decisions that I've made and their consequences. I hope to go easy on myself, I hope that you will go easy on me, and I hope you will go easy on yourself as you look over your own shoulder.

Since I started working on this project, I've dreaded writing about everything that comes after this intermission. Unpacking the experiences in the preceding chapters was cathartic; I've had enough time and distance from growing up in my hometown to have made peace with it. But most of what you will read in the rest of this book still feels fresh, even though some incidents have happened a decade (or more) ago.

Somehow, I thought that I could write about the things I've experienced without really talking about them. I literally thought about how I could tell stories without actually telling the story. How I could talk about the hurts without actually talking about them. Then I felt the Holy Spirit speak to me—"You can't be vague about the stuff that happened to you in this book you're writing"—and I realized that I had to be clear about my experiences.

Not long after that, someone recommended the book *Writing into the Wound* by Roxane Gay. It's all about writing into our personal trauma. Gay talks about how she "wrote around" a particularly devastating event in her life for a very long time.[1] She finally realized the freedom (and pain) that comes with just saying the thing. I want to just say the thing. But the idea of saying the thing feels incredibly exposing.

The following chapters might make you wanna cuss, cry, or slap the snot outta somebody because some of these folks were showing all the way out. I hope that as you read, you will be able to find yourself in these stories. I hope you will recognize that you are not alone. I hope you will come away with tools to help you stand against oppression. Most of all, I hope you will find your voice and that you will be set free to live as your most authentic self.

The source and site of most of the harm that I discuss in the following chapters was the white church. There are a few instances where I describe toxic religious beliefs and discuss aspects of my personal spirituality, but this book isn't a theological discussion because racism—though flagrantly perpetuated my many white

1. Roxane Gay, *Writing into the Wound: Understanding Trauma, Truth, and Language* (Scribd Originals, 2021), 7, Scribd.

Christians—is not a religious problem. Aspects of these stories could happen anywhere. I hope that you will keep this concept of "anywhereness" in your mind as you read.

I have remained Christian even after my experiences in the white church because I don't blame brown-skinned Jesus for white people's racist behavior. Racism is some white Jesus nonsense. For centuries, Black people have *chosen* to worship a God who promises freedom from oppression. I refuse to cede something to whiteness—something that didn't start with them and doesn't belong to them, by the way—that has brought me light, hope, and gives me the spiritual resources I need to free myself from oppression.

Although the names of people and places have been changed, and certain incidents and people made into composite sketches, it still feels incredibly exposing and vulnerable to say certain things "out loud." I have been "writing around" a lot of the nonsense that I've experienced for so long that I question whether I am able to say everything I need to say. I have self-edited for so long that I question whether the pain I felt was real or a figment of my imagination. I've tried for so long not to feel my feelings about these things, that I question whether I can adequately convey what happened.

Instead of writing around the pain, I'm going to "write my way out."[2]

2. Lin-Manuel Miranda, "Hurricane," *Hamilton: An American Musical*, Atlantic Records, 2015, MP3.

IF WHITE FOLKS DON'T DO NOTHING ELSE, THEY WILL MAKE SURE TO DO RACISM

6

FAKING THE FUNK (THE SACRIFICES WE MAKE)

When We Endure Racism Out of Self-Preservation

If I'd had any sense at all, I would've gone to a Black church when I went off to college. If I'd had any sense, I would've prioritized being in a church with people who looked like me over being in a church that believed all the same things that I believed at the time. Doctrinal differences are negotiable; one's dignity is not. But as the old saying goes, God looks after fools and babies. I was both.

After high school, I started college at Missouri State University in Springfield. Newly engaged to Ben, my high school sweetheart, I was enthusiastic for us to spread our wings, find our own church, and get involved in ministry. The one Black church in Springfield that was in my particular Pentecostal tradition felt too much like the churches I grew up attending, and so I decided I didn't want to go there (what with spreading my wings and all). We ended up landing at Living Streams, a predominantly white Pentecostal church that felt similar enough to the Black churches I had grown up in to be comfortable but new enough to make me feel as if I was making my own way in the world.

I had never attended a white church before and, given Springfield's reputation among a lot of Black Missourians for being a racist city, I was apprehensive about it at first. However, the church's pastor drew us in. Pastor _____ was a young, charismatic white man who preached the Bible with passion. In time, Living Streams truly became our church home. It helped that there was a Black family who were also members of the church. Seeing other Black people there made me think that it would be a safe place for me also.

In my youthful inexperience, I was eager to find my own path. Unfortunately, the path I found was a toll road.

I was excited to get involved in the life of my new church, and so I was elated when I was offered the opportunity to serve in the youth ministry at Living Streams. I felt called to ministry and working with teenagers was exactly what I wanted to do. After a while, I was asked to colead a new Sunday morning class for teenage girls.

I was happy about the opportunity to help lead the class, and I was excited to work with Dawn, my coleader. Dawn and I had served together in other areas of the youth ministry, and I was eager to learn from her. She had more than a decade of experience working with teens, and she was good at it. She prized authenticity and encouraged the young people to be themselves. I appreciated her approach because, as I was quickly learning, the white cultural tendency to prize conformity and avoid real talk applied even more stringently in the white church context. Dawn was one of the few people in the church who I felt I could be some version of my authentic self with, and I valued our budding friendship.

On our first Sunday teaching the class, a group of twenty or so teenage girls crowded into the tiny classroom. Dawn said that she would take the lead since this was the first week of the class. I sat back, eager to take mental notes on how she engaged with the youth. Her style was an offbeat combination of discussion, jokes, pithy commentary, and storytelling. The girls were giggling, joking, and hanging on Dawn's every word. I, the apprentice, beheld the artistry of the virtuoso.

And then it happened.

Dawn had a very animated face that she could contort into a variety of humorous expressions. Sensing a lull in the conversation, she decided to interject a bit of humor into the moment by making a weird face. She curled her razor-thin lips back onto themselves. Her mouth looked as if both lips had just been injected with lip fillers and stung by a swarm of angry hornets. It was as fascinating as it was grotesque. The girls erupted into laughter.

"Now I have lips like Ally," Dawn proclaimed through her up-turned lips as the initial burst of laughter died down. When the giggling resumed, Dawn continued to hold her pose like an expert comedienne waiting for the laughter to subside before moving on to her next bit.

Milliseconds after Dawn made her comment, one of the girls shouted, "You look like a monkey!" The girl gasped and then looked at me sheepishly (or was it devilishly?) and giggled when she realized the implication of her words.

The laughter that was rising in the room became choked and all eyes abruptly turned to me as the word *monkey* reverberated through the room. The mood was still lighthearted, though a few of the girls seemed to know enough to at least pretend to look shocked as they tried to hide their amusement.

I sat there, stunned. My heart was racing. I felt a flash of anger that I quickly pushed down as my face became hot and prickly. I felt utterly humiliated. I knew I couldn't reply without betraying how hurt I was. A soft trauma chuckle escaped my throat before I pulled myself together. I knew I had to be strong in that moment.

I mustered what was left of my dignity, gave my best Aunt Viv #1 side-eye, let out an "I'm too through" sigh, and looked away, trying to keep it together. I knew that if I showed how angry I felt, I would be "in the wrong." If I risked a clapback (like saying, "At least I have lips"), it could be seen as "disrespectful." If I acted hurt, I would be called "too sensitive" and reminded that it was "only a joke." So, instead, I sat there, bathed in humiliation and shame.

Dawn said nothing. It was as if she had simply commented on the weather.

I said nothing.

It took me ten years to even be able to speak of it, the shame I carried about the incident was so great. I couldn't find the words to talk about it. Not to another Black person. Not to my spouse. When I was finally able to talk about it, I technically didn't speak. I took a screenshot of a note that I had written on my phone and texted it to Ben because I was still too ashamed to say the words.

When Black people enter into white social spaces, we are expected to fake the funk. We are required to make adjustments to the way we move through the world so we don't run afoul of white sensibilities. We must pretend that we have never experienced racism or, if we have, that it was "somewhere else" and not "right here." We are required to pretend that we don't notice the insensitive comments, the rude assumptions, and the suspicion with which white people in the space treat us.

We are enlisted to preserve the illusion of white people's racial innocence—they have never said, done, or even thought anything that was remotely racist. We must adopt an "I'm just happy to be here" posture that doesn't offer any kind of substantive pushback, opposition, or correction to the status quo. Above all, we must never show our anger or engage in any expression that could be interpreted as angry. We must maintain these basic agreements if we wish to keep our place. It is a social contract signed in our Ancestors' blood.

We have all faked the funk with white people at some point. We've put on our best "customer service voice" so that the person we were talking to wouldn't have any reason not to grant our request. We've graciously ignored insensitive comments. We've kept our hands off our purse and out of our pockets while shopping. We've all made little sacrifices and accommodations to whiteness in order to survive. We can't be Sister Souljah in every situation, and anyone who says that they are is either lying or doesn't have to deal with white people in their day-to-day.

Those of us who regularly find ourselves in predominantly white spaces constantly choose between being our most authentic selves and being safe. We end up faking the funk as a means of self-preservation. Of course, this begs the question, Why not get out of these white spaces and go where Black people are? This is often easier said than done. People who live in rural areas or who reside in cities that have a small Black population would have to uproot their lives and move to places where there is minimal daily interaction with white folks. People cannot easily leave their jobs or other opportunities to be in Black spaces. Even changes that don't necessarily require moving, such as one's community involvements or religious affiliation, can present difficulties. We shouldn't have to leave anyway; white people should stop being racist.

A lot of times, we fake the funk because we struggle to imagine standing up for ourselves and telling white people that they are being racist toward us. We struggle to imagine what it would be like to confront the coworker who keeps calling us by the wrong name or telling off the Karen following us around the store. We convince ourselves that things could be much worse and use that as a reason not to push for the full measure of our dignity and freedom.

Sometimes racism is so normalized for us that faking the funk is all that we know. This was my situation. When Dawn turned her lips inside out in front of our class, all I could do was fake the funk. I didn't feel like I could express my hurt—my rage—at being humiliated in such a racist way. I could have confronted Dawn after the incident and told her how it made me feel, but I had no assurances that the situation wouldn't devolve into defensiveness, anger, or some other strong emotion that I would then be required to manage.

When you spend your life watching white people implode at the mere suggestion that they might have done something racist, you learn not to say anything to them about race or racism at all. When white authorities fail to address the racism in their institutions time after time, you learn to shut up. It is the epitome of the saying "once bitten, twice shy."

Being a superminority for my entire life taught me to accept experiencing racism as an inevitable part of living. It taught me that pushing back does very little because white people will always find a way to excuse their racism. I learned to find little ways to maintain a modicum of dignity, but most of the time I just absorbed the blows. I faked the funk and let them think they got the best of me because I couldn't bear the reproach of pointing out the worst in them.

The problem with faking the funk is that, when we do it enough, we can end up losing ourselves. It is another way that racism steals from us.

Racism is theft.

Theft of bodies.

Theft of wealth.

Theft of dignity.
Theft of place.
Theft of ideas.
Theft of labor.
Theft of culture.
Theft of opportunity.
Theft of the past.
Theft of the future.

Racism is the theft of our identities in service to white supremacy. Faking the funk is a coping mechanism that we use to survive racism, but faking the funk also threatens to steal our authenticity and our identities from us. When we fake the funk, we're being just that: fake. We can fake the funk and allow racism to keep stealing from us, or we can keep it real.

I think that keepin' it real gets a bad rap. Some people associate keepin' it real with self-defeating behavior that brings more trouble for a person than if they had left things alone (see also: when keepin' it real goes wrong). Others associate keepin' it real with individuals who use this term to excuse their toxic behavior. There are some who associate keepin' it real with "being loud" and so they make keepin' it real about respectability politics and try to police how other people decide to keep it real (see also: keeping it classy).

Keepin' it real doesn't have to be self-defeating or an expression of toxicity. It can be a tool that helps us reclaim our dignity when racism tries to steal it from us. We keep it real by being honest about racism and its personal impact. Instead of silently enduring indignity, we can boldly speak out. Instead of acquiescing to mistreatment, we can push back and say, "Thus far and no more." Instead of laughing to keep from crying, we can speak truth to power.

Yes, keepin' it real can be risky. We can't ignore the violence that white supremacy can inflict on our body, mind, and spirit. But we can't get free by faking the funk. Equality and liberation start with boldly pushing back against racism.

The one place where I haven't had to fake the funk is my marriage. Ben, who is naturally quiet and inquisitive, has always been eager to listen to me and empathize with my experiences. There has been the rare occasion where I've had to tell him that he's acting like an entire white man and that he needs to listen better, but he has always respected me. I've always felt that I could be my most authentic self with him. Ben knew from day one that being with me meant being with a loud Black woman, and he loves me *because of* who I am and not in spite of it.

This isn't always the case with interracial relationships. I've encountered a lot of Black people who entered interracial relationships under the pretense of "colorblindness" only to find out later that their partner is a racist. I've encountered a lot of Black people who got tired of faking the funk in their relationship only to find that their partner doesn't appreciate their newfound authenticity. It is lamentable when white spouses and partners flip the script and double down on whiteness, but I am wholly unsurprised when it happens.

Interracial relationships aren't and will never be the answer to ending racism. A lot of people who get into interracial relationships end up *avoiding* talking about race and racism (or they talk about it in unhelpful and counterproductive ways) because they haven't done the work to understand themselves, let alone the implications of their relationship. When people in interracial relationships have done the deep work of understanding their racial identities, they can be powerful agents of change. We don't see a whole lot of that because it is much easier and much more rewarding, particularly in Christian settings, to maintain the status quo.

I would like to tell y'all that I stopped volunteering with the youth ministry and that I left Living Streams after the racist incident with Dawn, but (as you've probably already guessed) I didn't leave. I should have left right then and there, but I was so used to faking the funk that leaving never even occurred to me. I knew what had happened was racist, but I thought that since I hadn't been excluded from anything or called a racial slur that it wasn't "that bad." I still believed that experiencing racism was an inescapable part of my Black existence, and so I continued to swallow and absorb the regular assaults on my dignity. The few times that I did try to tell people they were saying or doing something racist taught me that city folk were just as ignorant about racism as the people I grew up with out in the country.

In time, I would find my voice. But, as the Elders say, I had to "keep livin'" before I could gain the knowledge and the boldness to stop faking the funk and keep it real about racism.

7

BARACK OBAMA IS THE ANTICHRIST

*White Folks Don't Care If You
the Head Nigga in Charge*

Barack Obama's election was magical. It felt as if every Ancestor in the cloud of witnesses was smiling down on us. Every plate was perfectly seasoned. Every edge was laid. Every Afro was effervescent. Every knee was moisturized. For the first time in my life, I wondered if we might have made it to the mountaintop that Martin had seen. I was twenty-three years old and full of youthful idealism that caused me to believe Obama's election was the sign of a new day for Black people. In hindsight, the gains for Black people during the Obama administration were negligible, but at the time, his election imbued me with a sense of hope. I wanted to believe that things could change. I wanted to believe that things *would* change.

On election night, I called my mom and we cried. We were both in awe that there was a Black president. We laughed and reminisced about how in elementary school I wanted to be the first Black, woman president, an ambition that I had long abandoned. She told me that she never thought she would see a Black president in her lifetime and how she wished that Grandma was alive to see it. Then she told me something I had never heard, something she hadn't spoken of in thirty-five years.

Although she was the salutatorian of her high school graduating class, she wasn't allowed to give the traditional address at her graduation, presumably because she was Black. The rumor was that when the guidance counselor, a white man named Mr. Roy, told the school administration that it seemed like Mom might graduate second in her class, the administration did not want to give her the honor. Mr. Roy said that he would not tabulate grades for the rest of the class unless my mom would be named salutatorian if she earned it. The administration relented, and Mom received her honor. She still has the plaque that she received in honor of her achievement. For years it sat in a place of honor between her bachelor's and master's degrees, until Mom hung her degrees on the wall of her office at the same university that she didn't believe she'd have access to all those years ago.

For my mom, Obama's election represented a small vindication of the injustice of not being able to give her graduation speech. It was an indication of how far we had (supposedly) come in her lifetime. In that moment, we shared a sense of collective joy and hope for a better future.

That night, I fell asleep in front of the television as news commentators hailed the beginning of a post-racial America.

The morning after the election, I was still riding the wave of emotion from the previous night. I cried as I listened to the commentators on *Good Morning America* talk about the election. I cried as I gazed at the portrait of Martin Luther King Jr. that used to belong to my Aunt Becky, and I cried as I wondered what she and Grandma would say about our new Black president. I cried in the mirror as I did my hair for work.

I worked as the transportation director and high school youth pastor at Living Streams. I had started working there the week after Ben and I graduated (with honors) from Missouri State University. It was my first "big-girl job" after college, and I was eager to give every ounce of zeal and youthful energy to my work at the church.

I was the only Black person who worked there. Pastor _____ believed that Living Streams was called to be a multiethnic church, and he hired me as the church's first Black employee despite protest from a well-respected board member. I knew that my coworkers had probably voted for John McCain, but I didn't think that any of that mattered anymore. We were standing on the other side of a historic moment where political divisions seemed to melt away overnight. Did I mention that I was twenty-three years old and super idealistic?

I walked into my office that morning with an extra bounce in my step. I greeted Nancy, the secretary with whom I shared my office, with a big smile. I sat down in my chair and giddily pulled my laptop out of its bag and set it on my desk. As my clunky Dell laptop noisily booted up (this was years before I became a born-again Macintosh user), I waited for Nancy to say something to me. But she sat at her desk, clumsily working at her computer.

I'm not sure what I expected from her. Perhaps a simple acknowledgment of the moment we were living in? A hearty congratulations, maybe? At any rate, her dispassionate reciprocation of my greeting still hung in the air. Undeterred, I decided that I would be the one to bring it up.

"I can't believe that Obama won! This is such a historic moment," I said.

"I think he's the Antichrist," Nancy stated matter-of-factly, casually glancing in my direction with the kind of look you give somebody after sharing a juicy secret.

[Record-scratching noise]

I paused for a moment, waiting for her to say, "Sike!"

She did not say sike.

"I'm pretty sure that Barack Obama is not the Antichrist," I tried to reason. "Scripture tells us that a lot of stuff has to happen before the Antichrist appears."

"I still think he's the Antichrist," Nancy repeated.

I was spared having to come up with a response because Patrick and Nicole, two of our coworkers, burst into our office.

"Congratulations," Nicole said by way of greeting.

Finally, I thought.

"This must be such a big deal for you," Patrick said.

"Yes. It is," I said cautiously, afraid that Nancy was gonna start in on her nonsense again.

"I didn't vote for him, but I can appreciate that this must be such an important moment for you," Patrick replied.

"How do you feel?" Nicole pulled up a chair.

"I talked to my mom last night, and she told me that she never thought she would live to see a Black president," I began.

Choking back tears, I told them about how my parents grew up during the Civil Rights Movement. I told them about how Mom remembered how sad it was when MLK was shot. I told them about how my grandparents and older aunties and uncles were expected to cross the street when a white person approached them on the sidewalk. I told them about how Mom didn't get to give her speech in high school.

I usually tried to avoid talking about race with white people (my husband being the lone exception) because, more often than not, they would talk over me and try to tell me what my experiences were and what my experiences meant as if I wasn't the person living my life. Talking about race with white church folk was even more exhausting because they seemed wholly unable to sit with their discomfort about the topic and always wanted to explain it away as "sin" or individuals behaving poorly. But on that morning, something welled up within me and I tried so hard to tell the story of my people, *my* story.

"It's a really big deal for me. This is so important to me. I'm twenty-three. I knew that we would have a Black president in my lifetime. I just didn't think it would happen this soon," I concluded.

"I still think he's the Antichrist," Nancy stubbornly retorted, because white supremacy always insists on having the last word.

✦✦✦✦✦

If the Obama presidency did anything for Black people, it reinforced something that we have known all along: white people don't like being under Black leadership and authority. Many of them loved the idea of having a Black president that they could point to as evidence of America being "post-racial," but they were eerily quiet when time came to push back against the racism he and his family would endure. They loved the optics of having a Black man in the White House, but they caught Big Feelings when he attempted to lead and speak on the state of affairs in this nation *as a Black man*. Some of them were even quick to point out that his mama was white as if him being biracial negated their anti-Blackness. They wanted him to shut up [about being a Black man] and lead. Then, when he did lead, they made a point of questioning his leadership every step of the way.

When Nancy said she believed President Obama was the Antichrist, she wasn't just sharing a really bad theological opinion. She was communicating that she did not believe he could become president on his own merit and that there had to be some kind of sinister, supernatural power behind it. It was easier to believe his election was part of Satan's plan and not a function of democracy. Nancy probably wasn't the only white Christian to believe that

President Obama was the Antichrist, and she certainly wasn't the only white Christian to try to find fault with our first Black president based on flimsy claims (see also: Obama is a covert Muslim wanting to enact Sharia Law). Believing that he was the Antichrist gave her an excuse not to trust or respect his leadership as president.

Her sentiments were rooted in a racist disdain for Black leadership that led her to find an excuse—any old excuse—not to trust a Black leader. This was more than politics. If it were just politics, she would've been able to appreciate the historic moment for what it was. Labeling Obama as the Antichrist allowed her to spiritually bypass the moment and not have to contend with her contempt for having a Black president.

Integration taught white people that they merely needed to tolerate having Black folks in their spaces but that they were under no obligation to put us in positions of power. Later on, when the concept of diversity became *en vogue*, white people realized they could collect Black people to display as window dressing within their organizations while making minimal effort to ensure they were also giving Black people the opportunity to lead. As a result, white people have never learned to have any kind of regard for Black authority or to follow Black leadership.

This isn't to say that all Black leadership is good leadership or that all Black leaders are worth following simply because they are Black. The issue is that Black people in positions of power seem to draw sharper scrutiny and critique from white people. The bar for Black leaders is so much higher than it is for our white counterparts. Whether it is being elected president of the United States, serving on city council, leading a work project, or organizing snacks for the school Valentine's Day party, white people seem all too eager to check Black folks' qualifications, cast aspersions on how we came into power, doubt our ability to carry out our duties, and question our decision-making. There's always some kind of white noise trying to silence us and put us in our place.

Although no one called me the Antichrist (to my knowledge), I experienced this same type of questioning of my leadership during my time at Living Streams and in other positions that I've held in various predominantly white organizations. Leaders within the organization would recognize that I had a gift for leadership and would be eager for me to take on leadership roles. Then, when time came for me to lead, others within the organization (and sometimes the leaders that initially promoted me) would start to question my leadership. I'm not talking about the type of questioning and scrutiny that helps good leaders become more effective. It was much deeper than that. Not only did I have to demonstrate that I would continue to be an asset to the organization, I had to prove that I would not also be a liability.

Working within churches and faith-based nonprofits comes with the expectation that one will live and behave in ways that match the values of the organization. Church leaders are expected to operate with an extra level of virtue and to "lead by example." I always carried myself with the utmost integrity, always doing what I was required to do and abstaining from that which I was required to abstain. I never bent the rules and did my best not to do anything that could be seen as hypocritical. I wasn't just a Goody Two-shoes; I was a Goody Two-feet, legs, arms, butt cheeks, and everything else. I didn't even say cuss words back then. I did all of that, and people still treated me like I was suspect.

No matter how good I was at my job, no matter how virtuous I was, no matter how sincerely I worshiped and prayed at church, no matter how friendly my naturally shy and introverted self tried to be, I could not escape my Otherness. Being Other in white space means being perpetually dissected. Those with the most social power and privilege project their suspicions, doubts, and insecurities onto every aspect of your existence, and they will call you angry, defensive, and hostile when you disagree with their assessments. I frequently found myself cast as the angry, volatile Black woman who needed to be handled with kid gloves to ensure that I wouldn't be a problem. Pastor _____ was particularly adept at weaponizing these types of assessments of me.

I loved and deeply respected Pastor _____, and his opinion meant the world to me. He gave me opportunities that others in his position might not have, and I was expected to follow him with unquestioning loyalty in exchange. And for years I did, even when staying loyal meant being mistreated. There was one time that I disagreed with an assessment he had made about my feelings in a particular situation. When I shared my actual thoughts and feelings about the situation, he shouted at me and told me that he was right, then he continued to verbally berate me while I sat in stunned silence. Thankfully, the other pastors and ministry leaders I have served with were not as harsh and volatile as Pastor _____ could be, but I still experienced a lot of toxic leadership that tore at my self-esteem and left me questioning my perceptions of reality.

In addition to experiencing toxic leadership, I have also encountered damaging actions and attitudes from my colleagues at the various white churches and white-led nonprofits that I've been part of. Sometimes my colleagues would take it upon themselves to pull me aside to tell me how something that I said or did made them "feel uncomfortable" or upset them in some other way. Most of the time, however, they didn't tell me to my face. I would usually hear from a third party that I had upset or offended someone and that the injured party was too afraid to approach me to tell me about it. I heard about my supposed misdeeds through the grapevine so often that I thought about changing my name to Marvin Gaye. I am tenderhearted, and the thought of harming someone or people thinking that I meant them harm was particularly devastating for me.

When this first started happening to me, I rushed to make amends, assuming I was the one who did wrong. When I tried to seek clarity about my transgressions, my colleagues were rarely able to articulate what it was that upset them. I simply did something that made them feel some kind of way and they needed to tell me about it so that I could stop doing whatever it was. A few probing questions and time spent repeating back what they said usually revealed that their feelings arose from how they interpreted my actions and not from anything I actually did wrong.

My leadership woes often affected how I did my job. When I would give a directive, there were folks who felt the need to double-check what I said with one of my superiors. They could not accept that I had the authority to make requests of them and that I could be trusted to make decisions or act in the best interest of the organization. They would assume I didn't know what I was talking about or that I wasn't the architect of whatever program or strategy was being implemented. Interestingly enough, whenever I dispatched a white man to give a directive, people never seemed to question it and did exactly what they were asked to do without further prompting or conversation. I learned to adapt how I led certain people so that I could do my job with minimal pushback and stress.

I carried a persistent feeling of "damned if I do, damned if I don't." If I was assertive, I was taking up too much space and not "sharing" opportunities with others. When I attempted to delegate tasks, I was expecting too much from others. When I sacrificed my own effectiveness to make sure other people's teams were strong, I wasn't being a team player. If I stood up for myself, I had a chip on my shoulder. I was indispensable to the organization, but I couldn't give the appearance of having too much authority or operating within my sphere with too much autonomy. Whatever I did, it was both too much and not enough. Talk about mixed messages.

In his autobiography, *A Promised Land*, President Obama discusses how his administration made a point not to comment about the racist assumptions and rhetoric in which his opponents engaged. His reasoning for this was threefold. First, he made it a point not to publicly complain about criticism from voters. Second, his advisors thought it important that he not discuss race too much based on data from surveys that suggested white voters—even those who voted for him—did not want to feel like they were being lectured about racism in America. Third, he believed that because "racial attitudes were woven into every aspect of our nation's history," and since he could not discern people's motives with certainty, it was best for him to refrain from calling his opponents racist—even if his instincts told him differently.[1]

President Obama did what many of us have to do in order to survive in white-dominated spaces: we take on the burden of cultivating and managing a blameless image; we place white people's comfort above speaking our own truth; we tamp down our instincts; we don't trust ourselves; and we never, *ever* tell white people that they are racist. In essence, we accommodate white people and their racism in order to live at peace. Often, the cost of peace is our ability to speak up and name our experiences.

So many of us suffer alone and in silence, afraid to name our experiences and label them as racism. We struggle to name our experience for what it is because we don't want to be accused of "crying racism" or "playing the race card." We are bullied or gaslit into silence by the people and systems that do wrong by us. The fear of retribution pushes us to fake the funk and pretend that everything is all right. We are afraid that even if we do speak out, people will find fault with us and exonerate the people doing us harm.

Our own internalized racism pushes us into silence because we have been conditioned to distrust voices that are honest about racism and to spare the feelings of white people in the process. Respectability politics and assimilationist values guilt us into silence because we fear being seen as "militant" or being labeled as a "troublemaker." Silence, in turn, flings us into a chasm of

1. Barack Obama, *A Promised Land* (New York: Crown, 2020), 405–6.

isolation where fear, delusion, and shame make it hard to find the way out. And so we suffer alone and in silence.

The gag is that we're not actually alone.

There are other people who have the same kinds of experiences sitting with us in that chasm who also believe that they are alone. In fact, the chasm was designed to convince us of our isolation so that we would never use our voice and discover others like ourselves who can help us find our way out.

Thankfully, there have been settings in which I had other Black women serving with me in the trenches. I could breathe a little easier and lead more confidently knowing that there were people beside me who saw me in the fullness of my identity. They were a safe place where I could feel heard and understood, where I could reality test to see if my perceptions were correct and where I could get checked if I stepped outta line. Without my friendships with Black women, I would've given up on my dreams and my calling.

We all need people who will walk with us as we try to find our most authentic selves. We all need people who will be our champions, our defenders, and our prayer warriors. Once you find those people, never let them go.

When I think about Barack Obama's election, my mind usually wanders back to my office at Living Streams. I look back at my young, idealistic self, who was so proud to be breaking barriers, and I wish that I could tell her to focus on freeing herself instead of tearing down walls that white people built and then applauded themselves for dismantling. I would tell her that she can push back when white people say ignorant stuff to her. I would tell her that she doesn't have to stay anyplace where people are mistreating her. I would tell her being "the first" and "the only" can be a difficult and lonely existence, and that breaking barriers ain't all it's cracked up to be.

Integrating a space from which Black people have been historically excluded comes with experiencing the racism that kept us out to begin with. Leaders within the institution might say they "value diversity," but it doesn't mean they have plans to address the racist culture that denied us access in the first place. More often than not, they don't have any kind of plan to fight racism—just a vision statement and vibes. As a result, we're required to contend with a racist institutional culture that lacks self-awareness and has no mechanism to confront the harm inflicted within its walls.

If I could have a chat with twenty-three-year-old me, I would tell her that most of the opposition she's experiencing is because white people don't know how to follow Black leadership. I would reassure her that, while she has some growing to do as a leader, she's doing a good job and people's response to her isn't an accurate assessment of the quality and importance of her work. I would tell her she's not alone in her experiences.

I can't go back in time, but I can offer you the reassurances and affirmations I would give myself. You are worthy of dignity, gentleness, and kindness. You are not alone. You do not have to remain silent. There are others who are longing for your voice to reassure them that they are not alone either—all you have to do is speak up. Even if it makes white people uncomfortable. Even if your voice shakes. Speaking your truth is powerful, and the truth has the power to set you free.

Do you need any other affirmations? Write them down and regularly remind yourself.

8

KEEPIN' IT REAL

*Resisting Racism and Finding
Your Holy Hell No*

The work environment at Living Streams was toxic. Pastor ____, who could be moody and emotionally intense at the best of times, started to become increasingly unhealthy in his leadership. At the time, I didn't know the word *misogynoir* (racialized sexism); all I knew was that as the only Black woman on staff, I was often treated differently than the other staff members. I was not treated with the same gentleness and air of dignity and respect my (white) woman coworker was afforded, nor was I given the benefit of assumed competence automatically granted to the white men.

I received a lot of confusing messages about my leadership skills. One minute, Pastor ____ would praise me for my work. The next minute, I would receive stern feedback and questioning that indicated he didn't quite trust my decision-making. Then something else would happen and the cycle would start all over again. Young and eager to please, I internalized every bit of the stern "critique" I received from Pastor _____. Since some of the other leaders in the church treated me the same way, I believed that I was the problem and worked hard to prove myself.

I didn't have all of the knowledge and language to be able to fully name my experiences, but I started to suspect that people were treating me differently because I was a Black woman. Since I had accepted that experiencing racism was part of living, I didn't push back. I didn't push back, that is, until the day that I got fed up.

It was the first staff meeting after an F5 tornado hit Joplin, Missouri. I remember because the tornado was our main topic of conversation before Pastor _____ had a meltdown. He was frustrated because at our previous staff meeting, we all got up from the table without pushing in our chairs. He said it showed that we had become "departmental" in our thinking. He claimed that we often walked by trash without picking it up. My coworkers and I picked up bits of trash left around the church all the time, but it's possible we missed something here or there. Pastor _____ believed this showed a lack of concern for the church. He was sullen, his tone bitter and angry. I thought these were petty things to be upset about, but I kept my mouth shut.

At staff meetings, Pastor _____ frequently expressed deep feelings of frustration and humiliation at the slightest mistake or mishap that occurred during Sunday service. His feelings and their resulting moods became the staff's responsibility to mitigate; the tone of our meetings hung on whether he thought service the previous Sunday was up to scratch. All too often, Pastor _____'s frustrations with how the church service went devolved into criticizing individual staff members. At times, his indignation seemed to come out of the blue, making otherwise peaceful moments suddenly heavy and awkward.

After interrogating and scolding the two white male staff members for perceived deficits in their job performance, Pastor _____ skipped right over the white woman in the room and set his sights on me. He complained that a graphic I had posted to the church website was "weak." He claimed that my performance was weak because I wasn't managing my time well and cited the fact that I had traveled to Joplin, which is only an hour away from Springfield, earlier that week as evidence.

I was confused because I had done exactly what he asked me to do. He had approved the graphic at the previous staff meeting (a fact that a couple of my coworkers carefully pointed out). Another staff member had found the graphic in question through a Google search. I thought it was butt-ugly, but I posted it despite my personal objections because I didn't want Pastor _____ to accuse me of being "uppity" or "having a chip on [my] shoulder," like he had a few weeks earlier when I insisted on custom creating a graphic for our Easter service rather than using a premade graphic that was off message.

I was shocked that he had called me uppity. Where I come from, that is racially coded language and is utterly inappropriate for a white person to call a Black person. I don't know if he knew that, but I never heard him use that word to describe anyone else and so it didn't sit right with me. It also bothered me because calling me uppity played right into the Angry Black Woman stereotype. I was sick to death of being coded as angry and volatile when I disagreed with people or asserted a well-reasoned opinion.

My attempt to avoid experiencing misogynoir had backfired, and now I was being called on the carpet in front of God and everybody for something that I had done to keep the peace.

Indignant at having my work ethic questioned when I worked just as hard as anybody else in that room, I reiterated that he had approved the graphic in question, and I reminded him that I had gone to Joplin on *my time* and not his. I wasn't in Joplin when I was supposed to be working. Furthermore, I was helping with production, graphic design, managing the website and social media, leading youth ministry, and doing whatever else that was needed *without pay*. The church was struggling financially, and I had worked for two years without a paycheck—the only full-time staff member to do so. I continued to work without pay because, despite my best efforts, I could not land a paying job anywhere— likely due to the Great Recession. Besides, Pastor _____ promised to start paying me again when the church's finances stabilized.

He tried to tell me that I didn't have to talk about everything I did for the church without pay. I told him that, no, we were going to talk about it because he was trying to make it sound like I hadn't been working hard just because he didn't like what I produced. I refused to be made to feel guilty for taking time to do something I wanted to do.

I spoke calmly, trying to keep my tone measured even though I was ready to set it off. I worked to contain myself because I knew that if I matched energy, I would be the one who was wrong. My voice may have shaken, but it thoroughly conveyed that I was not about to take any more of his bullcrap.

Realizing that he had not only stepped in it but was also loud and wrong, Pastor _____ tried to walk his comments back. The damage was already done though. Pastor _____ questioning my work ethic was the straw that had broken my back. I had acted as a beast of burden in that church for years, spending countless hours helping build an institution that I believed in. Ben and I oriented our entire lives around Living Streams. We were always available and would drop everything to take care of anything that needed attention. Hell, we even bought a house on the same street as the church so we could be close to our church home. I did one thing that I wanted to do and now my entire work ethic was being called into question. Boy bye.

Mind you, I wasn't freaking out over this one thing. I wasn't taking someone else's bad day personally. There was an entire constellation of harms that led me to this moment, and when

I got there, I'd had enough. I was feeling the weight of holding that space as a Black woman. I was tired of being told that I was a highly competent leader and then not being treated like I was highly competent. I was tired of being measured on a different scale according to invisible criteria and then being told that I didn't measure up. I was tired of being treated like I was volatile because I broke unwritten rules. I was tired of being misunderstood and then called defensive whenever I tried to clarify my position. I was tired, and in that moment, I decided to stand up for myself. I have no regrets.

It was sheer happenstance (and perhaps a bit of Providence) that Ben and I had planned a vacation that started the day after Pastor ____'s meltdown. As we drove across country, I processed the pain that I was feeling. Ben, who is a great listener, held space for me as I gave myself permission to name what I had experienced for years at Living Streams. I had pretended to be unaffected by the racism and sexism that I encountered. I had rationalized the spiritual abuse. Our vacation was the first time that I was able to keep it real with myself after faking the funk for so long.

A lot of times, it is easier to fake the funk and project an aura of unbotheredness than it is to keep it real and confront people who will either get angry or claim to be victimized by our honesty about their racism. This is especially true when the people doing the harm claim that they care about us. It is much harder to address these issues with people we love and respect and believe also love and respect us. Sometimes, people who do harm really do think that they love us, but they love their dominance over us more, which is why they are often unwilling to do the hard work of addressing the harm they've done. Remaining present in relationships and associations where uneven power dynamics rule is a breeding ground for forming trauma bonds—the unhealthy connections that people sometimes form with their abusers.[1]

I believe that superminorities are particularly vulnerable to forming trauma bonds with white people who operate from frameworks of racial dominance. When white people create an environment where their racism and ignorance go unchallenged, the Black people in that environment learn that they must fake the funk so that they don't experience harm. Black folk who don't upset the status quo are seen as "one of the good ones" and are tokenized. The tokenized Black person is treated well, and so they form bonds of friendship and camaraderie with white people. The problem is that these bonds are predicated on everyone playing their designated roles; if the Black person steps out of their role, they run the risk of experiencing harm.

Faking the funk might work for a while, but it comes with a cost. Faking the funk cost me the ability to be honest about the harm that I experienced at Living Streams. Keepin' it real allowed me to begin to break the hold that toxic environment had on me and start the process of severing the trauma bonds that I had formed with people who exerted dominance over me. My voice might have shook, but so did the foundation of the prison that was holding me captive.

As the scales began to fall from my eyes, I realized that I could no longer remain at Living Streams. This revelation scared me—so much of my identity was tied up in being a leader at my church, and I wondered who I would be if I left. At the same time, I knew that staying meant I would continue to experience racism and spiritual abuse.

I told Ben that I thought it was time to leave Living Streams. He agreed. Neither of us had wanted to live in Missouri forever. During undergrad, we dreamed of moving to the East Coast and

1. Julie Nguyen, "What Is Trauma Bonding? 5 Signs & How to End the Abusive Relationship Dynamic," *Mind Body Green Relationships* (blog), last modified August 31, 2022, https://www.mindbodygreen.com/articles/trauma-bonding.

living either in or near a big city. We had put our dream on hold to serve Pastor ____'s vision at Living Streams, a vision that we believed was from God. Now, we allowed God to give us a vision for ourselves that wasn't connected to Living Streams or to Pastor ____. We were able to dream once more.

I had decided to leave Living Streams, but it would be years before I was free of it.

In my work as a racial justice advocate and public theologian, I regularly encounter Black people who come to the sudden, jarring realization that they have encountered racism in what was once a trusted space. A lot of times, these folks know that racism exists and can name previous experiences with racism, but they never expected the white people they trust to pop off on some racist nonsense. They are sometimes left uncertain about how to respond because they are afraid of what they might lose. They are afraid of losing friendships, their sense of community, their reputation, and their livelihood. They are afraid, and so they silently endure.

A lot of Black folks have a toxic relationship with white people that prevents us from keepin' it real with them and with ourselves. We might attempt to manage white people's feelings and behavior toward us. We might even anxiously spin and toil, trying to mitigate the next assault on our dignity and sense of well-being. Sometimes we fear what they can do to us, and so we accept mistreatment in exchange for a false sense of security.

When I think about my time at Living Streams, I knew that I had experienced racism there, but I was afraid of naming it as such as it was happening because I was afraid of the consequences. I was afraid I would be labeled a troublemaker, that I would lose opportunities, or that I would lose my place in that community. I couldn't see beyond my own fears, let alone be savvy enough to discern that it was a toxic environment (and that it was toxic beyond the racism and misogynoir). My unwillingness to keep it real—even if it was just with myself—stripped me of my voice.

Keepin' it real can be costly, and sometimes we are not always ready, willing, or able to pay up. Sometimes we rationalize our presence in harmful situations because we cannot clearly perceive what the next step of the journey is. We stick with the devil that we know because risk aversion keeps us bound to our sense of safety, even when we aren't truly safe. It takes courage to stand in your truth. It takes courage to find your voice and talk back to the harm. It takes courage to grab your purse and walk out the door when people are mistreating you.

Perhaps, what we need to push past our fears is a Holy Hell No (or an HHN, for those of y'all who don't want to cuss). A Holy Hell No is the feeling that rises up in your spirit and causes you to put a stake in the ground and shout, "Hell no!" A Holy Hell No is a boundary we ardently assert and don't allow anyone to violate without experiencing our wrath. Your Hell No is holy, not because it is spiritual (unless you want it to be), but because it is something that you cherish and guard.

Sometimes you have to cultivate your Holy Hell No because it doesn't always come naturally. Those of us who are prone to people-pleasing, who are "fixers," or who have had to endure a lot of adverse experiences might struggle with the idea of asserting strong boundaries. Cultivating a Holy Hell No is important because it can serve as a crucial alarm that lets us know when it is time to get out of an unhealthy situation. Oh, how I wish I had cultivated a Holy Hell No when I was in my twenties; it would have saved me a lot of trouble and heartache.

Your Holy Hell No is a powerful tool of resistance. Cultivating it is a matter of trust. Whether you place that trust in yourself or in a higher power makes no difference to me. Just trust in *something* that allows you to see beyond your present situation and gives you the hope that you no longer need to remain silent in the face of oppression.

When the unhealthy environment at Living Streams got to be too much for me to bear, it was a Holy Hell No that rose up within me and allowed me to push back. Saying yes to my Holy Hell No is what ultimately set me on the path to liberation. It would take time for me to mature in using my Holy Hell No, but it served me well in that moment.

What would it look like if we stopped rationalizing our experiences with racism? What would it mean to acknowledge our own toxic relationships with white people? What would it look like to prioritize our freedom over white people's opinion of us? What would it look like to be honest, even if it is only with ourselves, about the hurts that we are holding?

The good news is that liberation is a process. We don't have to have it all figured out at once. We don't have to force ourselves to take on anything that doesn't feel authentic. Freedom is something we attain in a moment and spend the rest of our lives growing into. The moment you decide that you no longer want to shove yourself into boxes constructed by white supremacy, you are free. Once you realize you are free, there is a process of recognizing the chains still dangling behind you. As you find your voice, you can start to remove those chains one by one.

Keepin' it real is the first step you must take on the journey to finding your voice. You can't find your voice until you stop faking the funk. You can't experience freedom until you recognize the chains that are holding you. Sometimes, people are afraid to keep it real because they are afraid of who or what they might lose. They fear the consequences, and so they try to be free while wearing the same old chains. Your chains will only keep you in the same place, attached to the same racism that is harming you. That ain't freedom.

Finding your voice is a journey, but you cannot make that journey until you take the first step.

9

STONEWALL JACKSON, HEAR OUR PRAYERS

When "Trying" to Fight Racism
Goes Horribly Wrong

After I decided to start keepin' it real about the racism I faced at Living Streams, Ben and I realized that a change of scenery was in order. We met with Pastor _____ and told him we believed our time at Living Streams was up and that we felt that Northern Virginia was calling us. We didn't have the courage to keep it real about how his behavior toward me had been the catalyst for our decision but the reason we did give was truthful.

A few months later, we stuffed as many of our possessions as we could into our vehicles and a tiny shipping crate and set out on a cross-country trek from our house in Missouri to a townhouse in Northern Virginia. Ben, who is a software developer by trade, secured a job in an office on Pennsylvania Avenue in Washington, DC. Burnt-out and wounded, I spent my days in deep prayer and reflection on our years in Springfield. I would return to full-time ministry eventually, but those early days in Virginia served as a much-needed season of healing.

⬡⬡⬡⬡⬡

When we arrived in Virginia, we connected with a ministry called SoulCry. We were drawn to the ministry's emphasis on prayer and worship and were excited by its racial diversity. Although the ministry was predominantly white, there were also many Indigenous, Black, Latine, and Asian people there. Arriving at SoulCry was the first time that I walked into a white space and didn't immediately put up my guard because the diversity made me feel at home. I didn't feel like I was integrating the church; I could just show up as me.

One of the things I liked about SoulCry was its "justice mandate," which meant, at least on paper, that the ministry was committed to racial justice (among other justice causes). Having a justice mandate led the leaders of the ministry to preach messages about racial justice and host conferences on the topic. They frequently talked about the justice mandate, and their calls for racial justice received hearty agreement and enthusiastic applause from people in the SoulCry community. For a lot of the people in the ministry, the conferences, messages, and justice mandate seemed to serve as evidence of their individual racial innocence.

To their credit, a lot of the white people at SoulCry were "trying," to some degree, not to be racist. The problem is that when white people "try" not to be racist, it usually means that they are willing to engage in racial justice theatre while making little substantive change to their hearts, minds, ethics, and institutions.

⬡⬡⬡⬡⬡

If we polled white people, most of them would say that they aren't racist. There are some white folks who are loudly and proudly racist, but most of them try to convince us (and themselves) that they aren't racist. They cite their presence in diverse communities, their religious or social affiliations, or that enigmatic "Black friend" that they all seem to have but for which they are rarely able to produce proof of life. Occasionally, they might admit to having racist thoughts or agreeing with racist ideas at some point in their lives, but they are quick to let us know that those things are deep in their past. Some of them might admit to having a racist relative, but they will do everything to disassociate themselves from that person and from racism in general.

If you asked them whether they were part of racist institutions or whether there was racism in their community, a lot of them would tell you no. White folks will stand ten toes down in their white flight suburb, redlined neighborhood, white Jesus–worshiping church, or segregated school in a gerrymandered political district on land that was stolen from Indigenous peoples and tell us that they will "fight against racism—*if* it shows up here." White people struggle to discern the presence of racism in their world, but they know it is something they should be against. And so they "try" to fight racism.

A lot of white people in white-led institutions treat racism like it is a subject they can revisit from time to time as part of a do-good checklist. They host seminars, acknowledge important days, write statements, and even make sure there are a plurality of skin colors in leadership. These are often good faith efforts that bespeak a basic level of awareness and concern. They are "trying." The problem with "trying" (and why I put it in scare quotes) is that white people's "trying" often lacks the level of commitment and substance needed in order to be effective. "Trying" becomes a hamster wheel on which energy is expended but forward motion isn't achieved. If we aren't careful, we can end up on the hamster wheel right along with them, chasing the elusive goal of "diversity" and "justice" because we settle for white people "trying" to do right instead of them actually doing right.

At SoulCry, the justice mandate was the centerpiece of the ministry's "trying." The mandate was cited as evidence that the leadership (and by extension the people participating in the ministry) cared about racial justice. At first, I felt encouraged that the ministry had a justice mandate. Up until that point, I had never encountered a white church that included pursuing justice as part of its mission. I eventually realized, however, that the justice mandate was nothing more than a nebulous idea. There was no substance to it.

The problem was that people of color had minimal involvement in shaping and implementing the justice mandate. It was the white-dominated senior leadership team who dictated what constituted injustice, what justice seeking entailed, and what justice looked like. Had the white leaders at SoulCry released their stranglehold on authority and listened to the perspectives of the people of color who participated in the ministry, they could have confronted their own biases and avoided promoting racist beliefs within the ministry, but they didn't. Their choices added to the constellation of harms that people of color, particularly Black people, experienced at SoulCry.

Being in a new community in a different part of the country, I tried hard to check my assumptions and patiently observe my surroundings. As I observed the people at SoulCry, it became apparent to me that they placed a high value on creating a context in which people could grow and deepen their sense of spirituality. I also observed that SoulCry was a community of storytellers and that the stories the community told to and about itself shaped its worldview and sense of purpose in the world. As a community of spiritual storytellers, the people at SoulCry placed tremendous value on crafting narratives to help them explain how they believed the Holy Spirit was speaking to their community.

A short time after we connected with SoulCry, a new story line started to take shape. The ministry's leadership believed that God was going to cause SoulCry and other churches in Virginia to experience a tremendous amount of growth in membership and that people would experience both physical and spiritual healing—all we had to do was pray for it to happen. At first, I was hyped about the idea of people making a positive connection with Christian spirituality, especially since so many people had been harmed by Christians. I became uneasy, however, when American history—particularly the Civil War—became a tool to support the narrative.

It started when SoulCry began gearing up for its annual prayer and worship conference that drew people from across the mid-Atlantic region of the country. In preparation for the conference, leaders of nationally known ministries visited SoulCry and reinforced what our leadership was saying. They also added two new, critical components.

First, God was going to use the prayers of the people in SoulCry, and other ministries in Virginia, as a catalyst for spiritual renewal across the United States (and even the world). According to the leaders, Virginians' prayers carried special spiritual authority with God since, as the first colony, Virginia was the "womb of the nation." They believed that our prayers could "birth" a powerful spiritual renewal.

Second, the leaders claimed that the United States was at a critical moral crossroads that was similar to the moral crossroads that gave rise to the Civil War. They believed there were many similarities between the United States during the Civil War and the United States in 2012. Specifically, a critical election that could decide the moral and spiritual fate of the nation.

As the conference drew closer, the narrative grew and became more complex until suddenly, abortion was being compared to the supposedly "innocent" bloodshed during the Civil War. People compared Barack Obama to Abraham Lincoln and said we should pray that Obama would abolish *Roe v. Wade* like Lincoln had abolished slavery. Leaders from SoulCry toured historic Civil War sites across Virginia and wove what they learned on these tours into talking points used to generate interest in the conference, which had grown into a national event with an anticipated attendance of ten thousand people.

As the Civil War played an increasing role in the narrative, I was surprised by how little race and racism factored into what the leadership believed God was speaking to the ministry. Trayvon Martin had just been killed, and the outrage over his killing was growing, but God didn't seem to be talking about the implications of a Black kid being shot for carrying a bag of Skittles and a can of tea. The only thing the Almighty seemed to be concerned with was chiding Black Americans for their abortion rate and comparing the nation's first Black president to a man who cared more about preserving the union than he did about the people who were enslaved in a supposedly free country. It seemed that God was anointing the Civil War allegory to serve the purpose of "birthing revival in America," but not to make people look more closely at America's original sin of racism.

The scope of the conference grew, and the prayers the Soul-Cry community prayed together started incorporating conference talking points. There were prayers asking God to make Virginia a womb for spiritual revival in the same way that Virginia was the womb for our nation. There were prayers asking God to make President Obama into another Abraham Lincoln. There was even a prayer invoking Stonewall Jackson. Yes, *that* Stonewall Jackson.

Confederate General Thomas J. "Stonewall" Jackson got his nickname during the Battle of First Manassas when another general, seeing how determined Jackson was to keep standing while catching a beatdown, shouted, "There stands Jackson like a stone wall. Rally behind the Virginians!"[1] The Confederate forces rallied and won the battle. Thomas J. Jackson would be known as Stonewall Jackson from that day forward. He would go on to become the poster child for winning the battle but losing the war.

One hundred and fifty years later, "Rally around the Virginians"[2] became an informal slogan for the SoulCry community and the upcoming conference. People across the nation in SoulCry's sphere of influence were given the spiritual injunction to "rally around the Virginians." The story of how Jackson earned his nickname was recounted countless times to reinforce the idea that God was going to use the prayers of people like us to bring about his purposes for America; all we had to do was stand firm—like a stone wall. For real. Some of the Black staff members offered pushback to the use of Jackson and the Civil War in the ministry's narrative, but their concerns seemed to be disregarded as the narrative grew.

Although the leaders were usually careful to qualify their comments with how they believed that Jackson was on the "wrong side" of the war, I was still disturbed that we were using a dude who fought to enslave my Ancestors (many of whom were enslaved in Virginia) as a model for anything, much less prayer. One thing I had learned during my short time in Virginia was that history in general, and Civil War history particularly, was embedded in everything. You can hardly swing a stick without hitting something that was named after some Confederate or a "founding father." It seemed that SoulCry's leaders were perpetuating the state's culture of awkwardly decrying, yet still elevating, its troubling history.

At first, I thought the leaders were speaking allegorically and using cultural touchpoints to help communicate what they believed God was saying to them. This might have been true to some extent,

1. "The Battle of First Manassas (First Bull Run)," National Park Service, accessed October 23, 2022, https://www.nps.gov/mana/learn/historyculture/first-manassas.htm.

2. There are some versions of the quote that say "rally round the Virginians" or "rally on the Virginians."

but it was also apparent (especially as certain big-name leaders got involved) that Christian nationalism and GOP politics had begun to overtake the narrative. This didn't sit right with me, but I pushed my feelings aside because I was used to disagreeing with most of the political opinions I heard in white church settings.

The call to rally around the Virginians had mostly been shared in sermons and as part of conference messaging. However, during one of our weekly prayer meetings, the prayer leader prayed that God would inspire people from across the nation to "rally around the Virginians."

The worship team took the prayer and made it into a spontaneous chorus that went:

> There stands Jackson like a stone wall
> Rally around the Virginians!

As the worship team sang the chorus, the room erupted with shouts of praise. People sang along with all their might. Worship flags waved. People jumped, danced, clapped, and shed prayerful tears. Everyone except the Black folks in the room seemed to be brought into a fit of spiritual ecstasy as Stonewall Jackson's name reverberated through the prayer room. It seemed as if white Jesus himself had endorsed the prayer as people caught the Holy Ghost and waved their Bibles in agreement.

I was shook.

I looked at the screen where the song lyrics and choruses were projected to make sure I was hearing right. I looked around the room to make sure I was seeing right. I had only been part of SoulCry for a few short months, and I didn't feel like I knew any of the Black people there well enough to attempt to give them the "what is this white nonsense" look, so I stared at the screen. I decided to close my eyes, pray my own prayers, and ignore what was going on around me.

The prayer bothered me, but I had yet to fully cultivate my Holy Hell No. I still believed it was my responsibility to absorb white people's racism rather than confront it, and so I didn't push back. The Stonewall Jackson prayer taught me that even when white people "try" to fight racism, they will still do racist stuff and attempt to normalize it instead of confronting their racism.

White-led institutions "trying" to fight racism is the biggest hustle that white people have tried to perpetrate on Black folks since forty acres and a mule. Don't get me wrong—white people need to deal with their racism, *especially* the institutional kind. The problem is that white-led institutions will often "try to fight racism" without doing the basic work of identifying the ways the institution promotes and normalizes white supremacy. An institution that struggles to identify white supremacy can't possibly combat it, and an institution that attempts to normalize white supremacy isn't trying to change anything.

Instead of addressing their racism, people in white-led institutions will try to silence us by making it seem like we are doing something wrong by offering pushback. Since they are "trying," people in the institution don't want to hear about how their efforts aren't working. "We aren't perfect" becomes a salve the institution applies to the wounds it inflicts as if the absence of perfection is supposed to make experiencing white supremacy hurt less.

"Trying" silences us by requiring us to accept mistreatment in the name of "learning," "growth," and false "unity." Requiring people to accept mistreatment is how white-led institutions normalize racism. When people normalize racism, it creates the conditions for you to believe that you can't push back. When people in white-led institutions try to silence you with their "trying," you don't have to shut up. You don't have to put your head down and accept anything less than justice.

When you find yourself being silenced in white-led institutions that are "trying to fight racism," there are a few questions you should ask yourself.

First, is it possible to leave the institution? You might not be able to leave your job or transfer out of a degree program, but you can leave a club, community organization, church, or other institution where your livelihood is not contingent upon your participation. If you are able to leave, try to find an institution that will better suit your needs.

If you are unable to leave an institution, you should ask yourself questions to try to identify the source of the silencing. Is it the leadership of the institution? Is it the rank-and-file people in the institution who are doing the silencing? Is it the institution's policies or procedures? Identifying the source of the silencing will help you better understand how you might speak up about your experiences.

Once you identify who or what might be silencing you, ask yourself how you might cut through the white noise and break your silence. Is there a formal grievance process you can enter? Or, if not, can you put it into writing anyway, to ensure your experiences will not be erased? Even if the process sucks, it is helpful to document that you went through it.

Are there people who are having similar experiences who you can partner with to bring attention to the issue? Are there people in positions of power who might be willing to break solidarity with power to help you seek justice? What do you want the institution to change? How do you want them to change it? What can you do to push back against the status quo? What is your exit strategy should the institution attempt to terminate your involvement (i.e., fire you, kick you out, take legal action, etc.)?

It sucks that we have to jump through extra hoops to ensure that we don't get harmed or mistreated, but I am sharing this so you can have the freedom of knowing you don't have to stay in environments that seek to shut you up.

After SoulCry's conference, the Civil War story line faded into the background until it was rarely, if ever, invoked in the ministry's narrative. Eventually, the leadership learned to tell better stories.

Many years after the Stonewall Jackson prayer, a Black woman who was on staff at SoulCry during the Stonewall Jackson period posted a status to Facebook sharing the pain and frustration she felt on that night. I was among a small group of people who were there at the time who expressed our feelings about the experience. Another Black staff member spoke up and said that she had tried to speak out about the prayer and about some of the other things that had happened in the ministry at that time. She shared her own pain over what happened and expressed that she should have done more.

The people who were responsible for setting the chorus, as well as the leader of the ministry, responded to the post, publicly apologizing for their part in what happened and denouncing their actions. I appreciated that they apologized, but I also think that apologizing is the bare minimum anyone could have done, especially a decade later. I hope that one day, SoulCry will truly live into its justice mandate.

I'm happy that someone spoke out about the Stonewall Jackson prayer, even if it was almost a decade later. It is never too late to break the silence.

10

FINDING MY VOICE

Learning to Push Back against Injustice

When I was growing up, I was a bit of a tomboy (and still am). As much as I loved each of my aunties, I relished the opportunities that I got to be around my three uncles: Pootie, Bear, and Aubrey. My uncles are my aunties' husbands; I never had the pleasure of knowing Freddie and Marvin, my mom's brothers who passed away before I could know them. At family gatherings, I used to listen to my uncles and my older boy cousins as they would talk about sports, fishing, and their lives in general.

Sitting at my uncles' feet is one of the first places where I learned about racism and how to begin to put language to my experiences as a Black person. My uncles and big cousins shared their thoughts and experiences so casually that I never fully appreciated just how influential those discussions were on my formation until years later when the time came for me to find my voice and speak out about my own experiences with racism.

In August of 2014, Ben and I were still living in Northern Virginia. We had a beautiful four-month-old daughter named Ezra who was commanding most of our time and attention, as infants tend to do. We were still part of SoulCry, but I was not in vocational ministry at the time; I had decided that I wanted to spend time at home with my new baby. My days were filled with changing diapers, giving bottles, folding laundry (babies make a lot of laundry), and watching *Downton Abbey* on repeat. I was doing one or the other of these things when I learned that an eighteen-year-old Black kid in Ferguson, Missouri, was killed by a police officer and that his body laid in the street for hours.

I spent a lot of time on social media between feedings and diapers, and so I caught wind of what had happened before the story went viral. At first, only a few people were talking about the incident on Twitter. As activists mobilized and more details became available, my timeline was soon filled with the hashtag #BlackLivesMatter and commentary on the incident. It felt like Trayvon Martin all over again.

It was upsetting to hear about one more Black child killed because the color of his skin made him an instant suspect. The years I spent listening to my uncles and big cousins talk about their experiences and observations as Black men in America taught me about the accommodations Black men and boys make in order to avoid white violence: The gentle tones they must adopt in disagreements. The patience they cultivate with being called "boy," even as a grown man. The reassertion of dignity to themselves and to one another after experiencing racism. The unwritten rules of survival that require sharp instincts as much as they do knowledge. On August 9, 2014, Michael Brown did not make the right kind of accommodations and so he paid with his life.

The Ferguson Uprising, as it would later be called, eventually went viral and became the main subject of discourse in the public square. I couldn't help but notice how differently Black people seemed to be processing this incident from everyone else, particularly white people. It seemed as if we were inhabiting two parallel, but totally different, realities.

White people seemed to only care about the "facts" of the situation and wanted to discuss everything they thought Michael Brown did wrong. Many of them put Brown on trial and argued why they believed his killing was justified. They pontificated about obeying the law and about obeying police officers. There was little nuance, empathy, or listening. Even white people who were sympathetic to the protests were focused on debating the facts of the situation while glossing over the pain that many people in the Black community felt.

Black folks, on the other hand, tended to take the facts of the situation into consideration and analyze them in terms of the broader implications for Black people in America. We tended to see Brown's shooting through the lens of our history in this country. We lamented the indignity of a child's body lying bleeding and uncovered in the middle of the street for four hours. We could see our brothers, cousins, and ourselves in Brown's slain body. In Brown's killing we saw all the times we've been stopped by police, all the times we've "fit the description," and all the times we've lost loved ones to the alleged "justice" system.

As a born and bred Missourian, my deep roots in the Show-Me State ensured that I had a front-row seat to every bit of racism-laced foolishness that a significant number of the white people back home had to offer. People I had known and been in community with for years suddenly became unabashedly racist. To be sure, white folks all over the country were wilin', but that Missouri racism hit different for me.

People from the Greater St. Louis area who lived nowhere near Ferguson threatened to shoot anyone they saw "acting like animals" in their neighborhood. They suddenly cared about the destruction of a McDonald's in the hood that they would have been too scared to eat at on a normal day. People who lived in other parts of the state joked about committing violence against Black people while simultaneously decrying the supposed violence of the protests.

I watched supposedly "born-again" Christians who were active in their churches express their agreement with statuses and memes that were so racist, I felt soiled after scrolling past them. I watched Sunday school teachers, church elders, worship team members, and other people who were prominent in their church communities make dehumanizing comments about Black people. I even saw a pastor post "pants up, don't loot," which was an ugly counter-assertion to the chant "hands up, don't shoot."

I was profoundly grieved that so many people I loved, valued, and respected morphed into something utterly unrecognizable overnight. What hurt the most, however, were the folks who remained graveyard silent when our mutual friends went on racist tirades. There was rarely any pushback, not even a mealymouthed "now, now, be nice."

Seeing so much ignorance hour after hour hurt. I didn't want to see, yet I couldn't look away. Sometimes I hollered at my phone, but I mostly prayed and cried.

I held my baby and cried as I watched the police's militarized response to the community unrest in Ferguson on the news one evening. As I watched Ferguson burn, I had one of the most important moments in my life. I realized we were in the early days of a new Civil Rights Movement and that the baby I held in my arms would grow up to read about it in her history books. One day, she would ask me where I was during that time and what I did, just as I had asked my mom about her childhood during the Civil Rights Movement of the 1950s and 1960s. I realized I couldn't tell my child that while Black kids' bodies laid like strange fruit in the middle of the street, I sat at home watching *Downton Abbey*. I wanted to do something, to make some kind of contribution to the moment that I realized our generation was in.

Remember when I talked about how it is important for us to identify our constellation of harms because it allows us to seek justice from a place of personal conviction? Remember when I talked about white noise, The Moment, being Unpretty, and all of the other things that threaten to shut us up? Remember when I talked about faking the funk and keepin' it real? Well, right here is where the rubber met the road and all of those ideas and concepts converged in my life, setting me on my current trajectory. Right here is where I fully found my Holy Hell No. Right here is where I decided I was no longer going to acquiesce to oppression. Right here is where I began to stage my own liberation. Right here is where I found my voice.

During the Ferguson Uprising, I shared my thoughts and analysis about race in America on social media. As Ferguson gave way to Laquan McDonald's killing, which then gave way to Tamir Rice, with many others in between, I continued to post about race and racism on social media. I tried hard to educate people out of their ignorance, and I was taken aback by just how invested in racism white people seemed to be. I spent countless hours going back and forth with people, pleading with them to stop being racist. Of course, they didn't like being called racist even though they had no problem acting the part. I pissed off a lot of people, and the number of friends I had on Facebook (and in real life) started to decrease.

I had received so much anger and pushback for sharing my views that it never occurred to me that people cared about anything I had to say, never mind that people would actually seek out my thoughts and opinions on race. Then one night, Ben popped the most life-changing question he'd asked me since his proposal a decade earlier, and it made me rethink how I viewed myself and my place in the world.

We were sitting at Applebee's enjoying an appetizer of spinach artichoke dip. CNN was playing on the television near our table, and I noticed that the feed had cut to a protest in New York. A grand jury had just failed to indict the police officer who killed Eric Garner.

"What does *The Armchair Commentary* have to say about all of this?" Ben asked, preparing a bottle for Ezra. *The Armchair Commentary* was the personal blog I had started a few months earlier. I mostly talked about parenthood, stuff that got on my nerves, and a little bit of pop culture commentary. Nothing too heavy or serious.

"Why would I post about this on my blog?" I asked, taking a bite of the dip.

"Because people would read it."

"Boy, ain't nobody tryna read what I have to say about this," I said, jerking my head toward the TV.

"People read what you have to say on Facebook."

"People read what I say on Facebook because they want to argue with me."

"But they're reading it. And you say a lot of important stuff that people want to hear."

"I don't know if they wanna hear it, but I'm still gone say it. I'm just not sure if my blog is the place for it. That seems like a lot of effort for something that people won't read."

In the weeks and months that followed our conversation, I started noticing that people really did seem to be paying attention to what I had to say. At church, people would stop me to chat about my latest post (sometimes to chastise me, but there were also several people who encouraged me to keep writing). The leadership at SoulCry invited me to be a panelist for a listening session they were holding for the senior leaders in the ministry. People would message me on social media to get my thoughts on something they had seen or read. Sometimes people would comment on my posts that they were waiting to hear what I had to say about the latest racial controversy or incident.

Ben was right; people really were paying attention to me. People were learning from me and viewing me as a trustworthy source for information and analysis. I realized that not only did I have a voice—my voice mattered.

Back then, I didn't have thousands of followers. I didn't have a podcast or access to other influential platforms. All I had was my keyboard and the resolve to make my corner of the world better. If racists could be loud and wrong, I was determined to be loud and right. I realized that I could combat the hateful things I was reading with messages of hope and truth that shouted into the void and commanded justice to come forth.

Finding your voice isn't about becoming a public speaker—it has nothing to do with the ability to speak well (or at all). Finding your voice is about setting yourself free from the weight of racism and refusing to assent to your own oppression. Finding your voice is about finding your most authentic self and not allowing that person to put their head down and absorb the blows dealt by white supremacy and racism any longer. When I found my voice, I also found my true self. I had faked the funk for so many years that I forgot what it meant to be *me*. I had locked myself inside boxes other people created for me in an attempt to hide parts of myself that I was told were too loud. I made myself smaller so that I wouldn't experience the sting of being both too much and not enough. Living your life in an effort to avoid being dealt harm ain't no kind of living.

A critical component of finding your voice is doing identity work. Understanding who you are, where you came from, and how these things impact your worldview is important to finding your unique voice. What are some of the strengths of your social location, and what are some things your social location might prevent you from understanding? What unique insight does the combination of your various identities bring to you?

Identity work is particularly important if you have spent significant time in predominantly white contexts because it's possible that you might have minimized aspects of your racial identity in order to "fit in." You might have some work to do to understand what impact racial identity subjugation has had on you. If you have spent your life ignoring or being silent about your identity, you might have to "play catch-up" to understand some of the experiences and concerns that people with your particular identity share.

Even if you have always had a strong sense of racial identity, it is still important to do identity work. It is important for us to understand the narratives and concerns that have shaped our people. Too many times, I have encountered people who are counterproductive to their own and others' liberation because they operate from outdated or unhelpful frameworks.

For example, a lot of Black folks were raised hearing things like "there's no race but the human race," "it don't matter if you're Black or white," and other maxims intended to emphasize humans' similarities to one another in an effort to encourage (white) people not to treat others according to harsh stereotypes. These ideas might have been helpful in their time, but most conscientious advocates for racial justice no longer agree with this approach because it has led to erasure, cultural appropriation, assimilation, and other things that fail to uplift Black people and serve to bolster white supremacy.

Outmoded tools for combating racism are ineffective, at best, and are often counterproductive. As the mechanisms of oppression evolve, so must the tools that we use to address them. What is important is that we don't undo one another's good work by giving white supremacy a foothold. This doesn't mean Black people have to be monolithic and think the same way about everything. We can work toward similar goals without everyone being required to do the same thing to get there; we can have unanimity without requiring uniformity.

Finding your voice doesn't require you to engage in public advocacy. It doesn't require you to build a public platform or create a social media following. For some people, advocacy might become full-time work that results in public opportunities and pay. But for most people, advocacy is an exercise in self and community care, which is what it should be foremost.

Our consumer-driven, capitalistic culture often seeks to monetize justice advocacy. We create unrealistic expectations about what it looks like to be an advocate and what it means to be "doing the work." We think that celebrity and notoriety are stamps of approval of our work. We think that gaining likes and follows means we have somehow made it. The question isn't how big of a platform we can build and how many eyes we can get on our latest thing. It is easy to fall into thinking that our effectiveness is measured by how many people are listening to us, when, really, the measure of our success is whether we are contributing to good in our community—whatever community looks like for you in our ever-connected and increasingly virtual world.

Finding your voice shouldn't be about amassing a following. It's not about marketing and speaking to a target audience. Finding your voice is about speaking the truth and allowing that truth to make you and those around you free. We aren't truly free if we are enslaved to the dictates of consumerism and capitalistic greed.

When I started speaking out about racism, it wasn't to gain a following or to become famous. Those still aren't my aims. I don't know why so many people care about anything I have to say. I don't know why I have a platform, but I have resolved to take what has come to me and do everything I can to make sure people are doing their best to create a more just world. If one day, people decide I am no longer worth listening to, I will die knowing that I did everything I could to push back against the injustice of racism and make the world just a little bit better for my children.

11

DIVERSE DON'T MEAN FREE

Dealing with Institutions That Consider Themselves to Be "Diverse"

"Things are a lot different now. I am a lot different," Pastor ____ said as a look of understanding seemed to pass between us. It had been five years since Ben and I left Living Streams. I had also changed a lot during that time, and so I wanted to believe him.

"It seems like a lot has changed here. It's good to see so much racial diversity," I replied, trying to find a comfortable sitting position in the chair Pastor ____ offered me as we sat down. I was pregnant with another little girl, Lysander, and being in the third trimester meant that I had reached new levels of physical discomfort.

"Living Streams is probably the most diverse church in Springfield now." Pastor ____ beamed with pride.

"That's great to hear, "I told him. "It's hard to have so much diversity in a city that is as white as Springfield is."

My family had returned to Missouri a few months earlier when I took a job at a small church in the Springfield area. I had also recently decided to pursue a Master of Divinity online at Fuller Seminary. I came to the realization that I couldn't be a youth pastor, seminarian, and mom to two little kids all at once, and so I decided to transition out of youth ministry and into a church where I could attend without being expected to lead.

Living Streams' newfound reputation as one of the most diverse churches in Springfield caused Ben and I to seriously consider returning. We requested a meeting with Pastor _____ to talk about the church. I wanted to get a read on what I could potentially expect if we chose to worship there. I didn't just get a read; I got an entire novel.

Our conversation seemed to be going great. Until it suddenly took a turn.

"I hope that I will be able to tell you to rein it in, if I need to," Pastor _____ said as the conversation shifted from catching up with one another to Ben and I returning to Living Streams. His tone was light, but the statement didn't feel light.

"What do you mean by that?" I asked, imitating his light tone but feeling quite taken aback by such a pointed statement. I could tell there was something behind his comment, and I wanted him to say it rather than be left to assume what he meant.

"During the election, this place became a powder keg. We had Trump supporters, and Hilary supporters, and even some people who came to church wearing Bernie Sanders shirts. The atmosphere made me nervous," he said.

I gave him a blank stare, which I hoped would encourage him to keep talking.

"We've worked hard for what we have here," Pastor _____ continued. "I don't want you to push me farther than I'm ready to go before I'm ready to go there. You know how you can be sometimes." He was trying to be funny with that last bit, but I didn't laugh.

"What do you mean by that?" I asked through a fake smile. I was starting to get the picture, but I wanted to hear him say it. He had built a house of cards that was nearly toppled by the tension of the recent election, and he was wary of anyone or anything that could send the whole thing tumbling down.

"I just want to be able to let you know if you're doing too much." He seemed to be saying that he wanted to be able to tell me to quiet down if my advocacy became too loud.

I wanted him to articulate exactly what the pain point was for him. "What do you mean by 'too much?'"

"I've heard that you're an activist now. . . . I don't want you to be an activist; I just want you to be you," he said. Back then, I self-identified as an activist. (I think the term *advocate* fits what I do a little better, but I didn't have all the words back then.) I used the term *activist* to describe the writing and teaching that I did about race and racism.

"And this is who I am," I said, gently. "My heart is reconciliation." I still used that term back then. "My heart is to bring healing, not cause problems." As soon as the words came out of my mouth, I regretted them. There isn't anything wrong with wanting to promote unity and healing, but I felt that my desire to be accepted caused me to resort to justifying myself, a huge regression on my part.

In the early days of using my voice, I felt a tremendous amount of pressure to cater to white people's feelings and sensibilities. I was so used to protecting white folks from the revelation of their own racism that I sometimes faltered between maintaining my reputation as a Safe Negro and keepin' it real.

White church contexts had taught me that "racial reconciliation" meant that Black people and white people were responsible for admitting equal complicity in the "race issue." I learned that solidarity among people of color meant admitting the ways we harmed one another but never collectively questioning white people's treatment of us. Black leaders in these contexts modeled acts of contrition such as repenting on behalf of all Black people for our collective "spirit of offense" about the racial terror that white people inflicted on us. I didn't actually believe God required me to admit fault in my own oppression, but I had hoped my "humility" would disarm white people's defensiveness and help them be able to listen and reckon with their own prejudices. What I found was that all my humble and contrite tone did was help them feel comfortable with me talking about race; it didn't encourage them to make any kind of substantive change. I had tried to show humility, but I ended up feeling humiliated.

I thought I had grown past the impulse to cater to white people's feelings, but the conversation with Pastor _____ showed me that I still had some work to do. The good news is that pushing back against injustice doesn't require us to have it all figured out at once. All we need is the willingness to evolve and the boldness to stand. I was proud of myself for standing, even if my words were imperfect.

As the conversation with Pastor _____ shifted to a lighter topic, I tried to remain breezy even though I was disconcerted by the turn that things had taken. It bothered me that he seemed to think I would come back to Living Streams and do anything that would harm the community or intentionally disrespect the labor of the people who had worked so hard to build the ministry. I forced myself to keep smiling like nothing was wrong.

Pastor _____ formally extended an invitation for Ben and me to return to Living Streams. As we left the meeting, I tried to project an air of positivity, but my spirit was troubled.

Oprah once said that the most important lesson Dr. Maya Angelou taught her was "when people show you who they are, believe them."[1] The Ancestors don't be lying, y'all. If I had believed Pastor ____ in that meeting, I woulda saved myself a whole world of hurt. But as my grandma used to say, "A hard head makes a soft ass every time." Again, the Ancestors don't be lying.

I felt some kind of way about the meeting with Pastor ____ and agonized about the decision to return to Living Streams. We had considered trying out some of the Black churches in town but eventually decided against it. Frankly, I was apprehensive about showing up to a Black church with Ben. I knew my family would be welcome at any Black church in Springfield, but I questioned whether bringing a white man into that space was the right move, especially in a city where there were so few places for Black folks to exist outside the white gaze.

We also considered trying out other churches, but the election of Donald Trump made me wary of what my family might experience. Living Streams seemed like the safest choice. I knew there were several well-respected leaders in the Black community who were outspoken about justice and also attended Living Streams. Their presence in the church made me wonder if, perhaps, I was misreading what had happened in the meeting.

"We don't have to go there," Ben said during one of our umpteen discussions about returning. "I don't think that I want to go back because it doesn't seem like it would be a good place for us." In addition to listening to the Ancestors, you should also listen to your partner because the Holy Ghost be speaking through them sometimes too. Ben is way more pragmatic than I am. His motto is, "If it doesn't make sense, don't do it." My motto is, "Okay, but what if we do it anyway? You know, just to make sure . . ."

So we went back to Living Streams, you know, just to make sure that I actually saw all of the red flags I thought I was seeing.

---

1. Oprah Winfrey Network (OWN), "One of the Most Important Lessons Dr. Maya Angelou Ever Taught Oprah," YouTube video, posted by "OWN," May 19, 2014, https://youtu.be/nJgmaHkcFP8.

Not long after we returned to Living Streams, it became quite evident that the church wasn't as far along as they believed they were when it came to race relations.

Pastor ____ was good at making bold, passionate declarations against racism that could elicit hearty "amens" from the congregation. The problem was that his declarations only challenged overt manifestations of racism and failed to push white people to consider their complicity in everyday racism. He frequently engaged in an unhelpful form of both sides–ism that implied racially marginalized people were equally to blame for the race problem in America.

When it came to anything involving racial justice advocacy at Living Streams, it became clear that Pastor ____'s voice was the only voice that mattered. The church was woefully unequipped to deal with the racism embedded in its culture. Pastor ____ grossly overestimated his ability to address racism in the church, and he grossly underestimated the amount of racism present within its walls.

As a result, there was an absence of overt racial conflict, but the church was rife with white people who behaved in ways that were insensitive to the needs and sensibilities of the racially marginalized people in the congregation. I watched Black folks literally grin and bear it when white members said insensitive stuff to them.

I recognized pretty quickly that my voice was out of the ordinary (and perhaps even a bit controversial) at Living Streams. I was pulled aside multiple times by people in the church who asked me if the leadership had "said anything" to me about my posts on social media and warned me that Pastor ____ or others in the church might have something to say. I always tried to graciously accept these warnings, but I was also unafraid of healthy conflict. Living Streams had a stated mission of racial justice, and I would hold the institution to that mission if it came down to it.

Living Streams was diverse, but I questioned whether the racially marginalized people there—especially Black people—were truly free.

I didn't feel free.

Diverse don't mean free.

It's easy for us to think that just because people tell us our skin color is welcome that the invitation also extends to our Blackness. There are a lot of supposedly "diverse" spaces that are fine with having a plethora of skin tones, but they only want the parts of our existence that make them comfortable and don't require divesting from white supremacy.

There are a lot of supposedly "diverse" institutions that love to collect Black folks like Beanie Babies. They display us on their shelves and pat themselves on the back for how great their collection is, but we are nothing more than props that they brandish while performing "woke" theatre. When it's time to take a stance against the racism that is "right here," and not just the racism "over there," they suddenly get stage fright and don't want to say anything. When Black people try to take the spotlight and speak up about our oppression, we are booed off the stage and told to shut up.

Diverse don't mean free.

All too often, white-led organizations treat racial diversity as a commodity that can be used to build the institution. They are fine with our slang as long as they can co-opt it to make themselves look cool, but when we bring our words and phrases with us into the classroom, boardroom, or pulpit, they start to question our fitness for leadership. They're fine with our clothes and our hairstyles when they can post pictures of us on their websites and social media, but if we're going to hold any position of power or influence, they want us to look more "professional." They can post #BlackLivesMatter on their socials, but when someone files a formal complaint about racism in the organization, they suddenly don't understand how racism works.

Diverse don't mean free.

A lot of organizations that pride themselves on their diversity are actually hotbeds of oppression because they continue to cater to the comfort of the most powerful instead of meeting the needs of oppressed people. They practice a cheap form of inclusion that comes at the expense of justice and requires marginalized folks to pay with their dignity. Such institutions tend to employ strategic silence as a way to support the institution's "diversity" optics while also maintaining the racial status quo.

Strategic silence is when an organization curates a justice-seeking public image by taking bold stances on things that are generally noncontroversial while remaining silent on things that could cause white people to feel unsettled. Being boldly outspoken on a noncontroversial issue purchases social capital that can be spent to placate marginalized people when the institution remains silent concerning more contentious issues. The institution will weigh the cost of remaining silent, knowing that if they are silent too frequently or regarding the wrong issues, they run the risk of hurting their diversity optics.

For example, on Martin Luther King Jr. Day, an organization might issue a statement saying they value racial equality, but that same organization will balk at the idea of flying a Black Lives Matter flag because they might not want to deal with backlash from the All Lives Matter people in their midst. They might even quietly tell leaders and influencers in the organization to refrain from wearing, posting, or otherwise promoting the phrase Black Lives Matter because they don't want to get "too political." When an institution cares only about the illusion of diversity and inclusion and not the reality, people in power within the institution will do whatever they can to maintain that illusion—even if it means doing harm to the very people they claim to care about.

When justice-seeking Black people in the organization try to point out the institution's weak stance on racial justice, the powers that be will work to shut them up. They will point to the institution's supposed "track record" and the diversity in the institution as evidence that they must be doing something "right." They will talk about how they are "trying" not to be racist. They will wring their hands and say, "We're not perfect." They will even truck out the institution's resident Safe Negro to chastise the other Ungrateful Negroes for making the Good White Folk feel bad about themselves and to reassure the white people in the organization that they aren't racist. The powers that be might even pretend to humbly listen to pushback, then decide not to change a thing.

Diverse don't mean free.

When interacting with an institution, whether it's a school, community organization, church, or even your place of work, there are a few things that can help you determine if the institution's diversity is only skin-deep. These suggestions are by no means exhaustive, but they will help you start evaluating your situation.

First, look at who is in power. Are there people of color in positions of power? Are they institutional "yes-people" or are they justice seeking? Are they using their influence to disrupt racism within the institution or are they using their influence for personal gain? Do they have a voice within the organization or are they window dressing? Are they opening doors for other marginalized folk or are they acting as a gatekeeper?

Second, try to get a sense of how people of color in the institution treat one another. Is there solidarity among racial minorities in the organization? Are the lines of communication between racial groups open? Do people of color engage in respectability politics and other forms of lateral oppression? Who is being tokenized, and are the token minorities engaging in respectability politics or other forms of lateral oppression?

Third, look at who is on the margins. Who is on the margins of the institution? Are they being silenced? If they are being silenced, why are they being silenced and by whom? If they are vocal, are people listening to them? Why are they on the margins in the first place? What, if anything, is being done to pull them from the margins into the center?

Fourth, look at the institution's commitments. Do they have a strategic plan for inclusion? Is it written down? Who created the strategic plan? What are its goals and how is success at meeting these goals measured? What is the organization's mission and vision for inclusion? What steps are they taking? To whom are they accountable?

Finally, look at the institution's rank and file. Are people of color free to bring their concerns to institutional leadership? How does the institution treat people of color who are gender and sexual minorities? How do they treat people of color who hold other marginalized identities? Are their concerns treated with care? Are people faking the funk? Are people afraid to be their full selves? Are there known affinity spaces for the various racial groups represented in the organization or do people have to gather on the low? Is the institution keeping people from being free?

Belonging to "diverse" institutions places a heavy load on Black people. If we aren't contending with white people's racism, we end up contending with anti-Blackness from other people of color. If we're not contending with anti-Blackness, we have to contend with other Black folk's internalized white supremacy and respectability politics. Because of the power dynamics that occur within and among racially marginalized groups, Black people—particularly Black gender minorities—often become the sole champions of change within an institution.

Bearing the load of white supremacy and racism in so-called "diverse" institutions that fail to directly confront their biases is heavy and heartbreaking work. We often struggle to balance the expectations of assimilation and our commitments to authenticity and justice. We are forced to navigate the troubled waters of organizational politics and unhealthy practices that threaten to silence our voices.

As I spent more time at Living Streams, I felt myself carrying an increasingly heavy load. Managing the pressures of being in an institution that promoted diversity at the expense of freedom was difficult. The leadership's strategic silence and racism within the church were frustrating, but I was determined to remain true to my voice. Eventually, the load would become too much to bear.

When you find yourself carrying the heavy load that comes with being in white-dominated institutions, don't be afraid to lay that burden down. Don't let the pressures of going along to get along convince you that you have to remain silent and oppressed. Do whatever it takes to remain true to yourself, even if it means leaving.

12

NO, I WON'T SHUT UP

Staying True to Your Voice and Message

Shut up.

There's something about those two words that can evoke a visceral reaction, at least for me. Perhaps it's because when I was a kid, saying shut up in front of my mom or grandma was like cussing—you didn't do it.

There's something about being told to shut up that feels like a sucker punch. It's mean. Humiliating. Hurtful. Your sense of indignation rises, and you want to retaliate.

Shut up.

Shut up and dribble.

Shut up and do your job.

Shut up and go home.

Shut up and go back to Africa.

There's something about being told to shut up that instantly strips you of power.

When you start using your voice, people will tell you to shut up. They don't want to hear your truth because it might force them to examine the unseemly parts of themselves that they try to keep hidden from the world. They will tell you that you're causing division. They will do everything they can to convince you that you're the problem. You can't worry about what these kinds of people think because their opinions don't matter. What matters is that you remain true to your voice and your message.

Using your voice comes with the responsibility of remaining true to the message that you have been entrusted with. There are going to be times when people will try to get you to second-guess that message. They will try to tell you that you are too loud. They will try to co-opt your voice and bend it to fit their agenda. When people attempt to get you off message, it is important to remember who you are and what you stand for and to surround yourself with people who will encourage you to be the best version of yourself.

As I became more confident in using my voice, my writing opened doors to speak and teach about race and grow in my racial justice advocacy. Along with more opportunities came more opposition and pushback. At first I took it all in stride, but then something happened that caused me to second-guess myself and whether I should continue with public advocacy.

May 19, 2018, was a red-letter day. Most people probably remember it as the day Prince Harry married Meghan Markle, but I will always remember it for two big reasons: (1) It was the day on which I received my first paycheck from a writing gig, and (2) it was the day that I almost quit racial justice advocacy. These things happened literally minutes apart.

I had just woken up from taking a nap after watching the royal wedding that morning. I was getting ready to work on the last assignments for my first year of seminary. As I settled down in my office, Ben came in, an excited look on his face.

"It looks like your paycheck came," he said, handing me an envelope.

Tears streamed from my eyes as I unfolded a check made out to me for $140. It was my first paid freelance gig, and I was over the moon. I had just finished drying my tears when my phone buzzed. It was a text message from my friend Ainsley. My heart skipped a beat.

The night before, Ainsley and I had a small dustup on Facebook. A mutual friend who attended Living Streams with Ainsley and I had posted that they didn't understand why people were upset that Donald Trump had called members of the MS-13 gang "animals."[1] I explained to this friend that racists often compare people of color to animals and that there were better ways to describe the gang's actions. The friend pushed back, still not understanding why it was wrong. I explained that as a white person, they might not fully understand just how hurtful being called an animal could be.

Ainsley jumped into the comments section and was angry that I would say that someone couldn't understand something just because they were white. She said that I was making something a "race issue" when it wasn't. I could tell by her comment that she was upset, and so I asked her what I could have said differently to not cause offense.

Mind you, I didn't actually think there was anything wrong with what I said, but I figured that if there was some way I could hit the trifecta of telling the truth, getting white people to listen, *and* avoiding offending folks, then the least she could do was tell me how. In my experience, doing all three of those things doesn't happen often, but I was willing to be proven wrong. I also hoped my question would help her recognize that she was upset about

1. Julie Hirschfeld Davis and Niraj Chokshi, "Trump Defends 'Animals' Remark, Saying It Referred to MS-13 Gang Members," *New York Times*, May 17, 2018, https://www.nytimes.com/2018/05/17/us/trump-animals-ms-13-gangs.html.

me saying the phrase "white people" so that she could deal with her feelings and realize that she was defending the dehumanization of Latin American folks.

When Ainsley texted me, she told me that she didn't know how I could have worded things differently. As blocks of text filled my screen, it became apparent that it wasn't the content of anything I said that was the issue. It was the tone that Ainsley inferred from my words.

She told me that my tone was "accusatory," my words were "harsh" and "cutting," and I made her "feel like an outsider." According to her, my social media posts "caused more division than healing," "did more harm than good," and "painted all white people as the enemy." She even pulled out the classic line, "If I said the same things you did, people would call me a racist." She was sure to let me know she wasn't the only one who thought these things. It was apparent that she had been stewing on her assessments of me for a while and was likely processing them with other people.

I was hurt by the things Ainsley said about me, but I was determined to stay true to my voice. I told her that I felt she was misunderstanding and mischaracterizing me. I shared my ethos in engaging in this work: I speak not to accuse but to make people aware of hurts so that we can heal. As she continued to push back, I tried to help her voice what exactly she was upset about. It was apparent to me that, for some reason, she was taking everything I said about white people in general as a personal attack. I tried to help her realize this on her own, but her Big Feelings kept getting in the way.

After some back and forth, it was clear we were not going to change each other's minds.

I put my phone down, my hands shaking from adrenaline. My heart was pounding as I tried to take slow, even breaths. I set my paycheck aside—it was still in my lap as I had texted her—and cried.

During my conversation with Ainsley, I felt bold in my resolve to remain true to my voice. But as I came down from the adrenaline rush, I started questioning myself. I know that my words can often be direct and seasoned with salt, but I also know the spirit in which I write. There were many people who said they appreciated my voice and that my words helped open their eyes. But was I missing the mark? Was I harming people?

Ainsley was my friend. I had known her and her family for years. I valued her thoughts and her friendship. I valued her perspective even when it was different from mine. I didn't want to do anything that would hurt her estimation of me. She said that my words were causing division. I didn't want to be divided from my friend. Ainsley had emphasized how much she loved and cared for me even as she said such hurtful things about me. She seemed to believe she was telling me hard truths, and I took her words to heart, though I disagreed with them.

Ainsley's words bored a hole in my chest. I felt deeply conflicted because, on the one hand, I had plenty of friends who seemed to affirm my work and encouraged me to use my voice, but on the other hand, I had a friend who was just as vocal in telling me I was doing harm. I feared that Ainsley was giving voice to something everyone else saw but was too afraid to tell me. I know that sounds absurd, but I cannot tell you how many times in my life that someone brought an issue to my attention only to later find out that other people thought the same thing but were too afraid to confront me about it. I was worried that this was another one of those times.

I decided to bring my concerns to a few of my friends who weren't connected to Ainsley. I showed them our conversation and asked for their honest feedback. Every single one of them disagreed with her and was quick to point out that Ainsley was engaging in tone policing and that she was bullying me. I also asked a few people who did not always agree with me or my advocacy for their honest feedback about my voice. They did not bring up the same criticisms or concerns as Ainsley and disagreed with her assessments of my tone. Gaining others' perspective was helpful, but I still didn't have peace.

I decided to dedicate some time to prayer and deep reflection. Prayer is an important tool for me. It is what keeps me grounded. It helps me find my "true north" and helps me operate with purpose and clarity. As I prayed and examined myself, I realized that my heart and spirit were broken. I felt heavy.

I had found my voice, and I was comfortable with who I was, but Ainsley's criticism had me wondering if, perhaps, I was doing something wrong by posting my thoughts on social media. I had just started my public Facebook page about six weeks earlier, and it was already starting to gain traction. Was there another avenue for advocacy I could pursue that wouldn't leave me hurting people I cared about? Was writing about race and racism on social media even something I was supposed to do?

I decided that I could no longer carry on posting my thoughts and commentary to social media for the time being. I needed space to evaluate myself and to evaluate my work and gauge if I was doing more harm than good. I resolved to set my social media advocacy aside until I felt peace to pick it back up again. In the meantime, I threw myself into my seminary studies and prayer.

As I prayed each day, my mind kept returning to an earlier lesson. As I grew into using my voice, I learned that white people seemed to feel stung by my words, no matter what I said. The only time they weren't stung by my words was when I bowed and scraped and acted deferential to them. Then they granted me permission to speak, but they were not behooved to change. When I catered to white people's feelings, I wasn't challenging them to change; I was reaffirming them in their complacency. When I did everything in the world to reassure people that they were nice white folks and that the only racists were the big mean guys wearing bedsheets, everything was cool. But as soon as my message shifted to "not just those people over there, but also you," folks caught Big Feelings.

Was Ainsley a faithful friend to whom I had done harm or was she someone who had caught Big Feelings because I had challenged her thinking and self-perception? I was pretty sure I knew the answer, but I wanted to be certain. As I prayed about continuing my racial justice advocacy, I prayed for God to shut every single door if I wasn't meant to do this work.

After a little more than a week of prayer and deep reflection, I felt a sense of peace wash over me. I still wasn't sure what role social media would play in my advocacy, but at least I wasn't experiencing the deep sadness and despair that I had been feeling. A few days later, it became abundantly clear that my social media advocacy was not only important but that people valued my voice in the racial justice advocacy sphere.

A student group I was part of at Fuller Seminary decided to organize a protest. We had been meeting with school administration for months to address concerns about racism in the institution. Our discussions with the administration reached an impasse, and so we decided to bring our concerns to the broader community.

Since I was good at social media, the team tasked me with organizing an online protest using the hashtags #SeminaryWhileBlack, #ToxicFuller, and #BlackExodus that two Black women who attended Fuller had originated. The movement gained traction and garnered attention from several national religious media outlets. Our protest resulted in Fuller taking action to address student concerns and changing aspects of the institution's culture. Our action also empowered students at other schools to push back against the racism in their institutions. Fuller still has work left to do, but I believe our protest moved the needle.

While the Fuller protest was happening, a friend connected me with Jessica, a pastor who was looking for team members to be part of a new church in Springfield. What my friend didn't know was that I was required to do a nine-month practicum for seminary, and it was getting close to time for me to find a practicum site. When I met Jessica, the first thing she said to me was that she had been reading my writer's page on Facebook and she loved my voice. I ended up doing my practicum at her church, and it was a formative experience for me.

Not long after I ended my social media hiatus, I had my first "viral" post. The post led Jemar Tisby and Tyler Burns to invite me to be a guest on *Pass the Mic*, a popular Black Christian podcast from The Witness Black Christian Collective. My interview on *Pass the Mic* led Jemar and Tyler to ask me to host my own show, and in April 2019, my podcast *Combing the Roots* premiered. I eventually became vice president of The Witness Black Christian Collective.

My social media posts also led to multiple literary agents contacting me and a publisher deciding to publish a book with my thoughts on racial justice. My presence on social media is why you are reading this book right now.

If I had listened to Ainsley, I probably would not be where I am today.

I was ready to quit, but it became abundantly clear that I was doing the right thing. I was willing to lay it all down if that was what was going to be the next right thing. I asked for every door to shut, but every single door opened. It could all be coincidence and happenstance, but I choose to believe that it was divine intervention that kept me from throwing away my future and placed me in the position to do exactly what I was supposed to do at the exact moment I was supposed to do it. I am exactly where I am supposed to be.

No, I won't shut up.

You don't have to shut up either.

There are going to be folks who don't like that you've found your voice, and they are going to do everything they can to bring you back to that place where you were faking the funk. They don't like that you're keepin' it real. They don't want to hear about the constellation of harms you have experienced that has brought you to where you're at right now. There are some folks who want you to keep faking the funk because they can exert control over you. They don't want you to keep it real because it might expose the ugliness inside of them. They want you to stay in the same old place: oppressed and silent about your pain.

Losses will come. There will be people who don't like the new you. There will be folks who don't like your new attitude and the confidence with which you speak your truth. But you can, and will, learn to manage those losses and live in the beauty of light and truth.

As we move into the third and final act, I hope that you will gain the confidence you need to take the next faithful steps on your journey to healing, liberation, and finding your voice. This is where your story begins. I will still share my story, but the next act is where I hope you will get what you need to confidently stand against injustice.

──INTERMISSION──

A LETTER TO MY CHILDREN

To My Most Precious and Most Special Children, Ezra and Lysander:

When I started this book, you were five and two years old. As I type the words on these pages, you are eight and five years old. You will be nine and six (or very close to it) the first time I read this letter to you. It took me a long time to write this book!

You might be wondering why I wrote a letter to you and why I put it in my book. I wanted to put a letter to you two in my book because you two are the reason why I am writing. One day, you will be old enough to read all of this book and better understand what that means. But what I want you to know right now is that I am trying to make the world a better place for you to live in. I hope my book helps makes the world a better place.

One day, you will read about the Black Lives Matter movement in your history books at school. You will read about how Black people stood up for our rights. I want you to know that I tried to be one of those people who stood up for my own rights, for your rights, and for the rights of other people.

Right now, there are a lot of people in the world who think that it's okay to be mean to Black people just because of the color of our skin. They think it is okay to say mean stuff about us, to keep us from voting, to keep Black kids from having good schools, and a bunch of other stuff that isn't very nice. I wrote this book to help Black people know that we don't have to be afraid to speak up for ourselves.

I hope that one day, when the opportunity comes, both of you will be able to use your voices to stand up for Black people's rights and to help lead our people to freedom.

There are also a lot of people in the world who love Black people and want to help us make the world a better place. I hope that if they read this book, it will teach them what they need to know to be good helpers.

No matter what, I will always love you both. I am proud of you, and I know that our Ancestors are proud of you too!

May our Lord Jesus Christ always lead you and may his Holy Spirit always bring you comfort and peace.

Love,
Mommy

ACT III

IT'S TIME TO GET FREE

13

YOU DON'T HAVE TO SHUT UP EITHER (LEAVE THEM ON READ)

How to Respond When People Try to Silence Your Voice

Nearly a year after I almost stepped down from my online platform, I received another message from Ainsley, the "friend" who told me that my social media platform was causing more division than healing. In her latest message, she said that she had been "listening"—whatever the heck that meant—but she had to unfriend me on Facebook because she was tired of being made to feel like she was racist. I was surprised to hear that she had been paying me any kind of attention since we hadn't interacted any more than awkwardly waving at each another in church for the past year.

A mutual friend had showed Ainsley a post that I shared on Instagram, and they were both very upset about it. The unnamed mutual told Ainsley she felt awkward seeing me at church and sometimes felt like she didn't want to be there when I was there. This revelation upset Ainsley, and so she decided to confront me about it and disconnect from me online.

Ainsley was angry and told me that I had violated something that she held dear: *her* church. The fact that she said Living Streams was *her* church really bothered me because it was also *my* church. My family and I made every effort to attend on a weekly basis even though I was also doing my seminary practicum at another church. She was doing some weird form of gatekeeping that was extremely petty and gross.

Ainsley was offended because I defined racism as prejudice + power and asserted that white people could not experience racism. I also said that anyone could experience prejudice and that people shouldn't be prejudiced, but she was obviously too full of rage to read for comprehension. Unfriending me was her way of putting her foot down. She told me I was full of hatred and said things that brought harm, and so she could no longer remain connected to me.

Sometimes you have to leave people exactly where they had you messed up.

I left her on read.

When you find your voice, all of the negative forces in this world will converge to try to get you to shut up again. There will always be somebody telling you that you're too loud. There will always be somebody trying to mischaracterize you. There will always be somebody who will try to twist your freedom into their oppression. As you become more comfortable in your own skin and start to touch new realms of freedom, there will always be somebody who will try to convince you that your progress has taken you too far and that you need to turn around and go back to where you were before.

The question is, Will you live into your freedom or will you let pushback send you back to faking the funk? When you experience pushback for using your voice, the first thing you should ask yourself is what the person pushing back has to gain from your silence. People will often come to you with "concerns" that are nothing but them projecting their fears, insecurities, narratives, and agenda onto you. They will frame their Big Feelings about what you have to say as concern for you. Some folks will even try to spiritualize it and blame white Jesus for them acting a fool. People who truly care about you will listen and hold space for you even if they disagree. They will listen to understand rather than listen to respond. They won't make threats, issue ultimatums, or use their emotions to coerce you into compliance.

I now see where Ainsley was not acting as a true friend even though she said she was. She came to the conversation placing her feelings and her offenses at the center. She took things personally that were not personal. She tried to hold me to account rather than hold space for me. Instead of asking questions, she chose to become defensive and lash out. If she were acting as a true friend, she would have first sought clarity from me about what I had said rather than port her own interpretations onto what I had to say. She didn't want to have a conversation; she wanted to make demands. She wanted to dump her feelings on me so that she didn't have to feel them.

People will come at you projecting their insecurities and accusing you of being hateful just because you're being honest. You don't have to take that into your spirit. It's okay to leave them on read.

When they call you angry—leave them on read.

When they try to steal your joy—leave them on read.

When they call you divisive—leave them on read.

When they say that you're too loud—leave them on read.

When they try to shut you up—leave them on read.
LEAVE. THEM. ON. READ.

If you are a recovering Token or Safe Negro, expect people to weaponize their perceptions of your "goodness" against you. A common silencing tactic is "you've changed" or "you used to be so respectful and kind." Why do they always call us respectful? They will try to guilt you back into silence by making it about how you have not met their expectations for how you should carry yourself. They will accuse you of hating white people and of stirring up division. They will create entire narratives in their minds about you, your motives, and what you stand for. They will weaponize all of these things in an attempt to push you back into silence. You don't have to pay attention to any of it. You don't have to answer people in their foolishness unless it brings you life to do so. Leave them on read.

Unfortunately, white people are not the only ones who might have something to say about you finding your voice. There might be times when other Black people set out to silence you. There are some people who are afraid of too much freedom because they have so much internalized white supremacy that they can't imagine true equality. They lean on respectability politics as a means of survival and validation. A lot of times, they are afraid because they have seen the worst of toxic whiteness and know the harm that can come all too well. They fear harm and retribution, and so they silence people who speak out. I try not to judge people who are afraid, because white violence is real.

There are some Black people who will want to shut you up because your voice doesn't fit into their notion of respectability. They associate truth telling with "being loud" and "militant," and they perceive you as a threat to their comfort. They are happy with whatever crumbs fall from the table, and they will fiercely challenge anyone who they perceive as interfering with them getting ahead. There are people who will shush you because if you're *too* free, they may no longer benefit from their tokenism. White people might just decide to start treating Black folks right, and they might lose their place. There are some Black folk who care about themselves more than they do the collective of Black people, and so they will put their individual needs above making sure that we are all free and that we all eat. Not all skinfolk is kinfolk. Leave them on read.

Finding your voice is an opportunity to find yourself, whether it's for the first time or for the first time in a long time. Finding your voice is a specific moment in time when you decide to no longer be stuck in the mire of white supremacy and internalized racism. It is also a lifelong journey of truth telling and justice seeking. There are times when your truth telling might involve talking to other people and confronting white supremacy head-on, but most of this journey is one of seeking freedom for yourself and empowering others to experience liberation also. Liberation is a marathon, not a sprint.

When I was a sophomore in high school, I joined my school's cross-country team. I played basketball throughout elementary school and middle school and was fairly athletic. When I started cross-country, I quickly learned that distance running was much different than running up and down the basketball court. In basketball you run in intervals, and so it takes a different kind of conditioning than distance running where there are no periods of rest. I tried to approach distance running the same way I did sprinting on the basketball court. The results were disastrous—I couldn't even run a full mile, let alone the 3.1 miles that were required for races. I had to completely change my approach to running and work hard to earn my varsity letter in the sport.

Over the years, I have watched so many people try to run this racial justice marathon like it is a sprint. They come off the starting line at full tilt, ready to "dismantle," "interrogate," and "divest of" (or whatever buzzwords and jargon seem to resonate with them the most) any and everything that has even a hint of white supremacy. The problem is that a lot of things in this world are tied to or corrupted by white supremacy. People will collapse from exhaustion before ever reaching the finish line, and the finish line is much farther away than it appears. When folks come off the line sprinting, one of three things usually happens: they retreat into silence, burn out, or become jaded.

There are times in justice seeking where we might experience different aspects of each of these three things. Having moments where we feel burnt-out or jaded or times when we want to retreat is natural, even when we pace ourselves. But when we experience these feelings after trying to sprint and do too much at once, we can end up responding to our pain points in unhealthy or counterproductive ways.

People who retreat usually do so because they become overwhelmed when they recognize just how oppressive the world can be. They start to question everything and then they feel scared because they're questioning things they once took for granted. They gain too much knowledge and awareness too quickly and are unable to handle it. They find it easier to retreat into the life they once knew.

I used to know a woman who had never fully considered that the white people in her community could be racist until someone she knew publicly shared a very racist joke. The incident made her question everything and everyone to the point that she became suspicious and wanted to withdraw from all of her relationships with white people. She didn't like how those thoughts made her feel, and so she decided that she could no longer make the journey of truth telling and freedom seeking because she valued her relationships.

She equated pushing back against the racism that was present in her community with suspicion and bad feelings toward white people. She could not separate the feelings that arose from the knowledge she was gaining and the work of truth telling and freedom seeking. For her, truth telling meant harboring suspicion and ill will toward her white friends, and so she was unwilling to journey farther in seeking justice. I regret that I didn't have the kind of relationship with this woman that would have put me in the position to help guide her. There was so much about the antiracist task that she seemed to fundamentally misunderstand, and because she was so overwhelmed, she was unable to parse through her feelings and assumptions.

Sometimes people who retreat end up becoming counterproductive to the cause of fighting injustice. This wasn't the case for the woman I knew, but it is something that I've seen. Sometimes people come off the starting line too quickly, and they gain knowledge that they don't have the maturity to appropriately apply to their lives. They might misunderstand or misapply what they learn and end up hurting themselves or others. They feel the consequences of their mistakes, and so they retreat back into the waiting arms of whiteness. They assume their misunderstood or misapplied knowledge is the truth, and so they tell tales of their deliverance from "wokeness" and mischaracterize the work of people who are seeking justice and freedom.

If you feel yourself starting to retreat, try to pinpoint the source of your discomfort. What are your assumptions about this point of discomfort? Is it possible that you are creating or believing in a false dichotomy? Does the problem or issue that you perceive have to be all or nothing? Can you sit with your discomfort and hold it in tension with the freedom that you are seeking and the truth that you are trying to tell?

People who burn out usually do so because their newfound awareness causes them to try to bleed the white supremacy out of any and everything. They become overly scrupulous, refusing to participate in or enjoy everything they think could be "problematic." They fight every battle, going to the mat over every instance where white supremacy shows up with the same level of tenacity for each offense. Large or small, every incident or slight raises the threat level to DEFCON 1 and must be dispensed with. They struggle to give people a chance to learn or course-correct out of fear that they could be giving place to white supremacy. They adopt a form of fundamentalism that seems principled on the exterior but often ends in existential crisis.

They chop away at the white supremacy they discern in everything, and they end up experiencing a personal crisis because they've left nothing to anchor themselves to. Like the person who retreats, the knowledge they gain causes them to become overwhelmed. The difference is that, instead of retreating, they remain in the knowledge that they have but they become too exhausted and unsettled to continue the journey.

Some burnouts might make the journey in fits and starts, vacillating between periods of energized "work" and burnout. I have seen this particular pattern show up in people who try to build a platform as they are trying to learn and process their journey of freedom seeking. They externally process concepts that they are still growing in, sometimes making messes along the way. The demands of trying to get eyeballs on their work coupled with the demands of trying to develop one's sense of ethics become too much and result in burnout.

People who are in burnout cycles can cause problems when their perfectionism and scrupulosity make it hard for others who are on the journey to feel comfortable making mistakes or having differing opinions. We need to be able to collaborate with one another to cocreate a more just world. It is hard to do that with people who are unable to participate in healthy conflict or hold space for reasonable differences of opinion. It is helpful for people who are facing burnout to embrace nuance, grace, and harm reduction.

Embracing nuance means recognizing that white supremacy and harm exist virtually everywhere, and so we must approach the world with curiosity and use our imaginations to envision how to redeem the broken parts. We need wisdom to know what needs to burn without burning ourselves.

Embracing grace means extending grace to yourself and to others. As you extend grace to yourself, you recognize that you don't have to get everything right at all times. Try your best to act according to your ethics and give yourself room to make mistakes. As you extend this grace to yourself, also extend it to others.

Embracing harm reduction means doing what you can to reduce the amount of harm in the world. There are times when we have to embrace the least harmful thing so that we can become healthy enough to fully address harm. It's not possible to bleed the white supremacy out of everything all at once. We have to replace the white supremacy with something constructive, lest we become unmoored and throw ourselves into an existential crisis.

An existential crisis occurs when a person struggles to understand the purpose or meaning of their life and how everything around them fits into that meaning. In this particular instance, an existential crisis can lead a person to question what value there is in anything if they perceive white supremacy in everything. If they are not grounded in a set of ethics or principles that they can use as a touchstone, an existential crisis can become a place of decay rather than growth.

If you are experiencing burnout, try to pinpoint where you are carrying burdens that are too heavy for you in this phase of your development. Where are you struggling to hold things in tension? Where are you struggling to extend grace to yourself or to others?

Are you expecting perfection in a situation where the best that can be done right now is harm reduction?

People often become jaded after they've spent a long time seeking justice that has not yet come. People who become jaded might stop using their voice because they don't believe they are making a difference. They might become resigned to the presence of racism in society and decide that there is nothing they can do to help bring justice. Sometimes people who are jaded continue justice seeking, but they struggle to see the impact of their efforts. They don't retreat back to who they were before, nor do they possess the same anxious energy that leads to burnout. They are simply weatherworn from a long and difficult journey. One might say that they've lost their spark or the light in their eyes.

If you feel yourself becoming jaded, try to find the places where good is being done or where progress is being made. Think back to where you were when you started this journey and take stock of how far you have come. Take time for self-care and self-development. If you are engaged in public advocacy, take a step back and allow yourself to find your vision for a just world once again.

Ask yourself whether you are taking on burdens of change that are too heavy for you to bear alone. Are you trying to shoulder the weight of the world? Are you continuing to advocate in a space where your voice is not being heard? Are you trying to effect change in a space where you are no longer called or where you are no longer effective?

A healthy approach to justice seeking understands that change does not often come overnight. Most of the time, progress toward justice comes after a tremendous amount of unseen labor by justice seekers who are committed to the cause. Liberation is a lifelong journey. Sometimes, the journey moves quickly and we are able to look back and marvel over just how much progress we've made. Most of the time, the journey is slow and we wonder if we will ever see any progress. It shouldn't be this way, but this is the reality that we currently inhabit.

Seeking justice and making the journey toward freedom is best done within the context of community alongside other like-minded people. Fostering community with others can help us get back on course when we try to retreat, experience burnout, or start to become jaded. I enormously value the little village that I have surrounded myself with over the years. We encourage one another, laugh and cry together, celebrate victories together, and speak difficult words of truth and life to each other when we fall short.

A hard lesson I have learned over the years is that you can't bring everyone along on the journey with you. There are going to be points when the path you're on forks and you must choose which way to go. When you choose a path, everyone in your community may not come with you. Some people will choose the other path. If you're lucky, you might once again cross paths with people who you once diverged from and you'll share tales and wisdom from the other side. You might journey together for a time and then diverge again. You might diverge from some of your community and never be on the same path with them again. And still there are others who see the fork in the road and decide they cannot make a choice, and so they will stay where they're at.

Breaking with people in your community can be a painful experience. It is hard when people decide they don't wish to make any forward progress. It becomes especially difficult when people who decide they cannot make the journey with us decide to mistreat us as they exit our lives. Leave them on read.

When Ainsley decided that she could no longer journey with me, I had to leave her exactly where she was. As upsetting as it was for someone I considered a friend to so grossly mischaracterize me, I realized that I could not be pulled into the back-and-forth of pleading with her to understand me when she was intent on misunderstanding me. I could not journey with someone who was more interested in commanding me and dictating that I keep her comfortable than in seeking understanding. She insisted on characterizing herself as the injured party while she responded with the same kind of anger and hatred she was accusing me of. White folks want to be oppressed so badly that they will manufacture oppression and then catch feelings over the problem they invented.

I hope Ainsley finds a friend, preferably another white woman, who will journey with her and help her do the work of becoming a justice seeker. I hope that friend is able to speak to her in a language she can hear and that she does the work of understanding her whiteness. I hope she will one day become a safe person for the Black people in her spiritual community. I hope no one else has to experience her bullying and her white rage. I hope that one day, she will be able to recognize just how foul her behavior was and that she won't treat anyone else the same way. But until then, I give her to God and leave her on read.

14

BE LOUD AND RIGHT

*Reclaiming Loudness and Using It
as an Oppression-Fighting Tool*

As part of my degree program at Fuller Seminary, I was required to do a ministry practicum during my second year. Jessica, a pastor who was starting a new church called Radiant Life, invited me to do my practicum at her church. I accepted the invitation with the understanding that my family would still continue to attend Living Streams.

I wanted to stay connected to Living Streams for two reasons. First, I didn't know what would come out of the practicum. I didn't know whether I would be offered a job there or if I would even want to stay. Second, since I didn't know what would come out of the practicum, I didn't want to unnecessarily create a sense of confusion or loss for my kids, because they loved the children's program at Living Streams. I figured that if anything changed, we could work through it then. Pastor Jessica was very supportive of my desire to put my family's needs first.

I spent the entire summer working with Pastor Jessica and the church launch team to prepare for Radiant Life to open its doors in September. The team consisted of about ten people and was mostly white, but there was another Black woman in the mix. Social justice was at the heart of Radiant Life, and our team had regular community discussions around a variety of topics, including poverty, racism, sexism, and Springfield's growing population of unhoused citizens. Pastor Jessica also preached sermons about social justice, and we prayed for the needs in our city, but we didn't stop there. What I liked about Radiant Life, and what set it apart from other ministries that I had been part of, is that we didn't just talk about justice—we tried to do justice. Our prayers had feet. During my time at the church, we partnered with other individuals and social justice organizations in Springfield. Where there were gaps, we leveraged our modest resources to help make a difference.

Pastor Jessica was also very supportive of my growing social media platform and regularly encouraged people to follow me. Jessica's ardent support was entirely different from the culture of strategic silence at Living Streams. Radiant Life was the first white-led institution I encountered where I didn't feel like I was pushing a boulder up a hill when I talked about race. It was a refreshing change, and my voice became stronger during my time there. I could tell that Pastor Jessica and the Radiant Life team were Good White Folks who were attempting to reckon with their privilege. Everyone was at different places in their journey, but I generally felt safe and included.

Of course, no situation is perfect. Even in situations where we encounter Good White Folks, something racist is bound to happen.

"We have a little situation that I want to make you aware of," Pastor Jessica stated after taking a long sip of coffee. "I think that it will be fine, but I didn't want you to be blindsided."

"That sounds ominous," I said, taking a sip of my chai latte. I'm not much of a coffee drinker, but Pastor Jessica—who worships coffee—insisted on having our weekly meetings at the Black-owned coffee shop on C-Street in Midtown Springfield.

"Remember when you talked about your *Black Panther* shirt during your greeting on Launch Day?" she asked.

"Sure," I replied, wondering where the conversation was going. During our first official church service, I had introduced myself to the congregation and shared that Radiant Life was a church where everyone was welcome. I had pointed to my outfit—a *Black Panther* shirt, head wrap, and jeans—as evidence that people were free to be who they are at Radiant Life.

"Well, I received an angry email about it from Ned," she said, searching my face for a reaction.

I blinked and cocked my head to the side. Ned was an older white gentleman who was part of the launch team. He had kind of a gruff exterior, but he was a nice guy once he warmed up to you. "Why was Ned upset about my shirt?"

"It took me a moment to figure that out. I ended up calling him. He was really upset that we would allow 'that kind of thing' into the church, and he said he wasn't sure if he wanted to be part of a church that would promote something so harmful. I couldn't understand why a Marvel movie would make someone so upset. Then I realized that he thought your shirt was promoting the Black Panther Party."

I burst out laughing.

"He ain't heard of *Black Panther*? It was only one of the biggest movies this year."

"No." Pastor Jessica chuckled. "I explained it to him and told him to go watch the movie on Netflix."

"I'm kinda bothered that he complained to you about it instead of talking to me about it. It kinda feels like he was wanting you to get me in line." I sighed. "I mean, I'm glad he didn't come to me because that conversation could've been harmful to me. But also, I'm an adult that doesn't need to be put in her place."

"Yeah, I can totally see where that would bother you."

"The other thing is, even if I *was* wearing a Black Panther Party shirt, he could've just asked why instead of being loud and wrong. The Black Panthers are a pretty basic part of Black history. It might have been helpful for him to try to get my perspective before going off."

"When have white people ever tried to understand something from Black people's perspective?" Pastor Jessica asked.

We both knew the answer.

The next week, Ned approached me after church.

"I owe you an apology," he began. "I made a judgment about you, and I was very uninformed. When you wore your *Black Panther* shirt, I didn't know what it was, and I was upset because I thought you were promoting the Black Panther Party. I grew up in Chicago during the '60s. I'm sorry. I got it wrong."

I could tell that Ned's apology was coming from a place of sincerity. My sense of discernment told me that this wasn't the time to try to educate him out of his misconceptions about the Black Panther Party, as much as I wanted to set him straight. He would have been a teenager when Fred Hampton was murdered and had probably only ever heard the whitewashed narrative about the work that the Black Panthers did.

Ned had been loud and wrong, and I wanted him to sit with the weight of his snap judgments and the feelings that he was carrying after realizing he was wrong. If I pushed back, the lesson might be lost and he would not be open to receive the learning that he still had to do.

"I can see where your experience might have shaped your opinion," I said. "I accept your apology."

On the grand scale of being loud and wrong, Ned's offense was relatively minor. There are a whole lot of people who have been louder and more wrong than he was in this situation. But this relatively minor (and somewhat humorous) situation goes to show us, once again, that racism can show up anywhere—even in places where people are actively trying to address their racism.

In stark contrast, there are people who have no qualms with being loud and wrong with their racism. They have no problem voting for racist policies and politicians. They have no problem showing up to school board meetings to fight against equity and inclusion. They have no problem sharing racist videos and memes on social media. They have no problem letting the world know what they think, and they are only getting bolder with their racism.

A large segment of the white population gives absolutely zero bothers about being loud and wrong. They don't care about looting people's rights, culture, dignity, wealth, and everything else from them, nor do they care about frameworks of oppression and justice-seeking paradigms. What they care about is the assertion and maintenance of white power. Racists have no problem being loud and wrong, and so we should do everything we can to be loud and right.

Black people often use the word *loud* to criticize how other Black folks decide to show up in the world. The concept of loudness in our community is multilayered. The most obvious layer is the volume at which a person speaks. Another layer involves how a person carries themself, including their clothing and other aesthetic choices. Certain class signifiers, such as a person's education level or what neighborhood they live in, also factor into what is considered loud. Anything that trends away from white, middle-class notions of "normal" is considered loud, even within our own communities. An additional layer involves how a person lives out their principles and ethics; anything that doesn't fit into mainstream religious or political ideology is considered loud.

When we use the term *loud* to describe other Black people, we are engaging in a politic that penalizes people for failing to ascribe to racist and classist notions of "appropriate" behavior and assigning value to their personhood. When we criticize people for being "loud," we're engaging in a form of respectability politics that prizes conforming to the racist status quo over freedom.

Respectability politicians stay calling folk loud, but they rarely try to understand why someone might be loud. Sometimes "loudness" is a response to being spoken over or silenced. This is true in our interpersonal relationships as well as in relation to the dynamics of oppression and liberation. Sure, there are times when folks are just being extra, but there are also plenty of times when a "loud" person just might have something to say. We can't tell the difference if we dismiss the message based on its delivery. We should be listening to one another instead of telling people to hush.

Black people need to reclaim the concept of loudness. Instead of trying to shove ourselves and everybody else into boxes that were crafted for our oppression, we should embrace the fullness and authenticity of who we are. Everything about ourselves that people try to tell us is loud and Unpretty, we should wear with pride. We should let go of oppressive frameworks that marginalize people based on their class, ability, gender, and other factors and acknowledge the worth that is found in our diversity. There are so many beautiful manifestations of Blackness that we miss out on when we dismiss them because we think they are too loud.

Being loud and right means boldly standing for the cause of freedom. As Ancestor Ella Baker told us, "We who believe in freedom cannot rest."[1] We who believe in freedom cannot rest because the devil stay busy. Every day, Black people experience harm in some shape, form, or fashion. It's easy to become overwhelmed by the presence of injustice in the world, but change won't happen until we make it. You have the power to create change by being loud and right.

You don't have to become a social justice superhero who fights against every wrong you perceive in the world. It's not humanly possible for one person to advocate for every cause out there, nor is it a reasonable use of one's energy and resources. Instead of trying to fix everything, find something that is important to you and do what you can to become an advocate for that cause. One of the best ways that you can create change is by connecting with other like-minded people. Joining advocacy groups (or building a group where none exists) is a good way to learn more about issues and work toward solutions.

Since injustice creates a constellation of harms, you are likely to find that your desire to advocate concerning a specific area might overlap with other similar issues. It's okay to partner with people whose advocacy might differ slightly from your own. A common mistake people make is becoming so siloed in their own causes that they miss opportunities to connect and build with others.

Being loud and right also means knowing what you're talking about. You don't have to be a scholar in order to be an effective advocate, but you should do what you can to acquire knowledge about your area of advocacy. There are many valid ways of gaining knowledge. You don't have to accept white supremacist notions of what it means to know and gain knowledge. Some people gain

1. Ella Baker, unnamed speech delivered on August 6, 1964, in Jackson, MS, quoted in Barbara Ransby, *Ella Baker and the Black Freedom Movement: A Radical Democratic Vision* (Chapel Hill: University of North Carolina Press, 2003), 335.

knowledge from books, while others gain knowledge from the streets. What's important is that you acquire knowledge from good sources and develop your critical thinking and analytical skills to the extent of your ability and capacity.

As you seek knowledge, keep in mind that you don't have to know everything. It's okay to rely on your community to help you learn. Gaining knowledge is a discipline best undertaken within a community. Spending time listening to people who know more about a topic than you do and asking them questions is one of the best ways that you can learn. Taking what you learn and trying to teach it to someone else is another great way to learn. Let your community teach you the best forms of advocacy for your cause.

Being loud and right will look different for everyone. For some people, being loud and right will look like engaging in public advocacy that puts them in front of people. For others, advocacy will look like operating in support roles that help sustain a grassroots group or large organization. Some people's advocacy might include fundraising, networking, and coalition building. Other people's advocacy might be cooking, washing dishes, and setting up chairs. Some people might advocate on Capitol Hill and others might advocate at the neighborhood watering hole. We need everyone. Everyone has value.

Wherever your advocacy takes you—whether it's standing in front of multitudes or sitting beside one—your work is valid. You have a voice. Never be afraid to be loud and right.

15

LETTING GO (WHITE PEOPLE NEED THEIR FEELINGS HURT)

When to Let Go of People Who Are Invested in Oppression

Finding your voice in a world that tries to silence you is both a learning and a growth process. You will probably make mistakes, say things you wish you could take back, and be forced to work through your own internalized white supremacy. You will likely also find yourself pushing back against the racism in the various institutions and structures in our society. People who were used to you faking the funk with them might catch Big Feelings when you start keepin' it real. You will have to learn to leave people on read when they remain intent on trying to silence you. All of these things are an irritating, yet necessary part of refining your voice. Another aspect of refining your voice is learning when to move on from individuals and institutions that remain invested in white dominance.

As you grow into using your voice, you might find yourself becoming increasingly frustrated with the people and places you had hoped your advocacy could transform. You might wonder what the threshold is for the amount of work that should be done in a space before it's time to cut your losses and go. Perhaps, you may even start to feel a bit conflicted about whether you should stick it out in a difficult place or if you should move on.

For a long time, I thought being an advocate meant that I had to bear with toxic people and institutions in the name of the elusive goals of "change" and "progress." I thought using my voice meant going back and forth with people who remained content with their ignorance. Being an advocate does require a high level of patience, but being patient with folks isn't the same as allowing them to string you along while they remain invested in their racism.

I give you permission here and now to leave anyone or any place that don't treat you right. You don't owe them shit. Not your voice. Not your time. Not your talent. Not one single thing on this earth or under the earth.

You don't have to stick with people or institutions that are intent on doing harm, especially when they have had ample time, learning opportunities, and encouragement to change. You don't have to play Captain Save-a-Racist. You don't have to let them harm you so that they can "learn" how to treat people with dignity and respect. You don't have to die on the cross to save white people from their racism. And if you moving on hurts their feelings, then boo-hoo. White people need their feelings hurt.

Toward the end of my practicum at Radiant Life, Pastor Jessica invited me to stay on as the church's associate pastor. Around the same time that Pastor Jessica extended her invitation, I was also invited to be part of a new antiracism initiative at Living Streams. I was conflicted about which opportunity to take, but I eventually decided on Living Streams because I thought it was the place where I could have the most impact. Radiant Life was a great church full of wonderful people, but doing racial justice advocacy there felt like I was preaching to the choir.

At this point, I was a sought-after speaker on the topic of racial justice and healing, both locally and nationally. My social platforms had taken off, my podcast was doing well, and I was booked and busy. I hadn't just found my voice; I was using it actively. I also had a strong desire to use my skills within the context of a local church. What would be better than helping to build a (long overdue) antiracism initiative in one of the most diverse churches in the city? I knew that I was walking into the center of a fiery furnace, but I carried with me a sense of hope that, maybe, things would be all right.

When my practicum was over, I said goodbye to the crew at Radiant Life and started worshiping full-time at Living Streams again. (I know, right?) And let me tell you, I picked a helluva time to come back. A few weeks after I agreed to join Living Streams' antiracism initiative, there was an incident that sent a shock wave through the Black community in the church.

A longtime and well-respected member shared a very racist video on social media one Sunday morning before church. It was bad. Like top-5 one of the vilest things I've seen in my life. Of course, the woman made all kinds of excuses for why she shared it, which only ended up doing more harm to the folks who tried to confront her about it.

A group of Black women met with Pastor _____ after the incident to share how we were impacted by what had happened and to ask that something, anything, be done about it. Pastor _____ told us that he watched the video and did not question its horribleness. He promised to speak with the woman about the incident. We were grateful that Pastor _____ was going to address the video, but this incident had touched a sore spot.

Several of the women shared years of frustrating and hurtful experiences with white people at Living Streams. They discussed things about the church's culture that concerned and frustrated them. I also shared my own experiences and observations about the church. I tried my best to stand alongside the women who were speaking up and lend my voice to the cry for healing and justice to come to Living Streams.

I could tell that Pastor _____ struggled with what he heard. He regularly lauded Living Streams for its diversity and took the presence of Black and Brown people in the congregation as evidence that the church was doing race relations right. Now, he had a group of Black women telling him that they were faltering under the weight of racism in the church. Many of the women had been faking the funk because they were caught between the racism they were experiencing and the hope of things changing. The video was a symptom of a bigger problem.

Although Pastor _____ recognized that he had a hot mess on his hands and that that could go left if he made the wrong move, he still felt the need to establish himself as the "authority" on race relations at the church. When we challenged some of his assertions and assumptions concerning race at Living Streams, he instantly became defensive. The church wasn't as far along on race as he believed, and that knowledge seemed to hurt his feelings.

White culture has set white people up for failure when it comes to dealing with racism. They are socialized not to discuss race and to expect Black people to cater to their discomfort with the topic. Gaining a basic level of competency in discussing race, let alone identifying racism, requires them to work against centuries of social programming. When they start taking the first tentative steps toward racial awareness, they don't want us to say or do anything that would hurt their feelings.

White people need their feelings hurt though. They need to hear the uncomfortable truth about their racism. When we cater to white folks' feelings instead of being up front with them about the impact of their racism, we communicate that their behavior is tolerable. They have no burden placed on them to change, and so they don't.

Far too often, Black people end up bearing the weight of healing and justice seeking in the wake of racist incidents. We have to navigate experiencing further harm or re-traumatization when white people double down on their actions. We are expected to manage the defensiveness of people who are unable to productively manage their racial discomfort. Sometimes we find that it's safer to fake the funk so that we can avoid experiencing further harm.

For a long time, I was overly concerned about hurting white people's feelings as I sought justice and healing. I took it to heart when they unloaded their rage on me, and I tried to find pleasant ways to help them understand racism. I eventually realized that I was enabling their racism while allowing them to harm me. I think that a lot of folks cater to white people's racial comfort because they conflate hurting someone's feelings with doing them harm.

The difference between hurt and harm is that hurt is temporary; harm is lasting. Some things hurt us in the short term but end up benefitting us in the long run. Getting an impacted wisdom tooth removed hurts, but the temporary pain of having a tooth removed is much better than the long-term harm that can be done if that tooth becomes infected. Similarly, someone's feelings being hurt because you refused to cater to their sense of racial comfort is much better than the harm associated with experiencing their racism.

We cannot continue to carry the burden of managing white people's emotions, even when it is a means of self-preservation. I am a firm believer that the truth can set people free. Speaking the truth is an act of imparting knowledge. White people can no longer claim ignorance when we drop knowledge on them. Speaking the truth about racial injustice is bound to hurt some white folks' feelings because they perceive your truth telling as an attack. You are not responsible for managing how they feel about what you say; you are responsible for telling the truth. And if the truth hurts their feelings, that ain't on you.

A month after our initial meeting, the group of Black women who met with Pastor _____ still hadn't received an update about what action had been taken with the church member who shared a racist video on social media. Simone, one of the women in our group, organized a follow-up meeting.

The meeting began with an update from Pastor _____. He had spoken with the woman about the video. She acknowledged her mistake and, according to him, she felt embarrassed and wanted him to do whatever he thought was necessary to bring closure to the situation. As far as Pastor _____ was concerned, the matter was finished, and so he got defensive when we started asking questions about what further action he planned to take.

The group expressed gratitude for the update, but the matter was not closed for us. We shared our thoughts and brought the conversation around to what was happening in the church as a whole. We offered our feedback on how the church could move forward. A majority of the women in the room specialized in some area of equity and inclusion, and we gave Pastor _____ a level of input that organizations pay big money for, for $FREE.99. What he did not seem to either understand or accept was that this was not an isolated incident, but rather emblematic of an undercurrent of racism that was quite active in our church. He continued to get defensive as we offered simple suggestions for improving our community.

"I think it would be helpful to have training for some of our key volunteers. It seems like a lot of people just don't know how to interact with people of color, and so they end up saying and doing hurtful stuff," I suggested.

"I can't put you in front of people because of your social media presence," Pastor _____ cut in. His tone indicated that he was trying to shut me down. Or perhaps it was to put me in my place? Or both?

"I'm fine with that. I never said that I had to be in front of anybody," I replied. "I'm perfectly content to help make a difference behind the scenes."

"But you haven't been here." He glowered.

"I was doing something that was *required* for my degree so I can graduate."

He knew good and well why I hadn't been worshiping at Living Streams full time, and he felt some type of way about it. We'd had a whole awkward conversation in which he reminded me about his early investment in me as a leader, and he told me that he hoped it "counted for something" when I started my practicum.

"Well, I just need to know that you're on my team." He huffed.

"I wouldn't be here if I weren't," I said. As the conversation shifted, I reflected on how Pastor _____'s response to me seemed unnecessarily combative. It reminded me of our staff meetings back in the day, which made me feel uneasy.

I wasn't the only one to experience Pastor _____'s combativeness. When Simone asked him to share his vision for race at Living Streams, he rounded on her like a junkyard dog protecting its favorite hubcap. He shared harsh things that other, unnamed people in the church had shared with him about her—including that she wanted to leave Living Streams. When Simone asked who was saying these things, Pastor _____ got loud with her. He shared a bunch of harsh assessments that were rife with misogynoir, including calling her angry and unapproachable. He told her she didn't have any influence in the church, which was particularly spiteful since Simone and her husband were pillars of the Black community at Living Streams. She attempted to stand up for herself, and they ended up in a full-blown, voices-raised argument. The rest of us looked on in horror.

I was hurt and disgusted by the unmitigated misogynoir that Pastor _____ displayed during the meeting. I emailed him later and shared how his behavior toward Simone had made me feel as a Black woman. I requested a meeting with him to discuss that and a few other issues that had arisen in the meeting. He responded that he wasn't able to meet, but he had "taken [my] words to heart." I was discouraged that we weren't able to meet, but I hoped his response was a sign that he was going to make things right with Simone.

I was horrified when Simone texted me a little more than a week later and said that Pastor _____ had "prayed about" her family's involvement at Living Streams and "thought it was best" that they "find another church." It was clear to me that they were being asked to leave the church, but it was being wrapped up in spiritual language. Simone and her husband were one of the most visible Black couples in the church and a lifeline for many of the Black members. Now they were being discarded.

I was shocked and confused by this turn of events. I wanted to respect the fact that Pastor _____ couldn't meet with me, but I also desired to understand what had happened with Simone. I decided to request a meeting with one of the other leaders in the church. The other leader agreed to sit down with me and suggested that I also reach out to Pastor _____ again.

I emailed Pastor _____ a second time and asked if he could meet with me to help me gain clarity on the matter. He said he was unable to meet and that it "became clear" to him that Simone and her family "would be best served under different leadership." He stated that he had nothing more to add. The next day, the leader I was set to meet with informed me that Pastor _____ had instructed church leadership not to discuss the situation.

Pastor _____'s actions confirmed what I had suspected but couldn't quite admit to myself until then: he had not changed at all.

I felt a Holy Hell No start to rise up within me.

First of all, I could not stomach the lack of integrity it takes to deny people pastoral care in service to covering up a leader's misdeeds. That's fertile ground for all kinds of wrongdoing. Second, I realized that I couldn't stay in a church where Black women could be treated so harshly while white folks could do racist crap with zero consequences. Simone experienced more consequences for standing up against misogynoir than the white woman did for sharing a racist video.

It was clear to me that, when faced with the choice of doing right by Black folks or keeping white people comfy, the leadership of Living Streams was more willing to discard Black people than to confront racism in the institution. I had to come to terms with the hard truth that a lot of people will say they don't want to be racist, but they will make choices that indicate they are not willing to let go of white power.

When people make these kinds of decisions, it's okay to call a spade a spade and leave. And that's exactly what I did.

As we work for change within white-dominated institutions, we have to know our limits and be clear with ourselves about what attitudes and behaviors are signs that we need to get off the train. It helps to decide this well in advance of having to make the decision. It is important to set boundaries in this regard because failing to do so can result in being drawn into unhealthy cycles of expending emotional labor and experiencing harm when things don't change. There are some questions that you can answer to help you get an idea of what boundaries you need to set.

First, what behaviors, policies, practices, etc., are a no-go for you? These aren't necessarily things that would make you grab your purse and go immediately, but rather things that would cause you to try to meet with leadership or lodge a formal complaint. For me, patterns of behavior are important. I expect white people to say and do racially insensitive things. What I look for is whether the rank-and-file people in an institution consistently engage in racism and are unresponsive to being corrected. I also look at the institution's culture. If the leadership caters to white people's feelings and struggles with accountability when racial incidents happen, that's a major red flag.

Second, are there stated timelines and benchmarks for progress? I approach timelines with the attitude that some progress is better than none, but too much incremental progress is the same as no progress. In other words, I will stay with an institution if there is a reasonable amount of continuing, visible progress, but I will start to reevaluate if change comes so slowly that it doesn't feel like anything is changing at all.

Third, what would cause you to hit the emergency eject button? That is, what type of situation would cause you to remove yourself from the institution quick, fast, and in a hurry? I will not continue to work within an institution that asks Black people to swallow indignity and penalizes them for speaking the truth while failing to hold white people accountable for their racism.

To the best of my knowledge, the woman who posted the racist video still worships at Living Streams. She experienced no visible, long-term consequences for her actions. She continues to be well-liked and respected in her community.

Simone and her family started attending a Black church in town. She and her family are thriving in a spiritual community where they are seen and valued.

After the incident, my family was embraced by several pastors, faith leaders, and congregations in Springfield. My family attended an Episcopal church in town for several months until we moved to Chicago at the beginning of the pandemic. I now attend a Black Episcopal church (becoming an Episcopalian is another story for another book).

Within two years of the incident, all of the women who met with Pastor _____ about the racist social media post stopped attending Living Streams for one reason or another.

I'm happy that I moved on from Living Streams. I hope that, one day, Pastor _____ will find it in himself to offer a wholehearted apology to each of the people who were in that room on that day and that Living Streams will become a justice-seeking church—not just nominally, but actually.

Letting go ain't easy. In fact, it can be downright heartbreaking, but you will be better for it.

16

LOSS MANAGEMENT (TROUBLE IN MY WAY)

Learning to Cope with the Losses That Finding Your Voice Can Create

If there is one thing that I wish somebody would have told me on this journey, it is that you will lose people, even people who you care about and believe care about you. Nobody told me that, and so I'm telling you, in case you don't already know. I had no idea that speaking up for people to have equal rights and dignity, especially in church, would mean I would lose friends and a sense of community.

In the advocacy circles I run in, we talk a lot about going where you're celebrated and not merely tolerated. We talk a lot about identifying and leaving places where you are unable to flourish. We talk about divesting from unjust systems, decentering whiteness, and decolonizing our minds. I don't think we talk enough about the losses that come with doing those things.

As I have become more engaged in advocacy over the years, I have learned that loss is a very common experience. It seems that those of us who wish to create a more just society end up losing something in the process. We lose friends, jobs, communities, places of worship, opportunities, and certain aspects of the life that we knew before speaking out. We lose things that are both tangible and intangible.

Seeking justice, it seems, is often full of loss.

Leaving Living Streams left me with a tremendous sense of loss even though I knew that it was the right thing to do. What I had to come to terms with, what I am *still* coming to terms with all these years later, is the harm that I experienced not only in that fateful meeting but also in the years of spiritual abuse that I endured while attending the church. Many things were unhealthy about the culture at Living Streams, but racism and misogynoir are what did the most harm to me and compounded all the other issues. Pastor _____ was not the only perpetrator, but he was the one who promoted a culture in which people were "not afraid to fight" to defend their sense of church unity, the vision of their leadership, and their understanding of the gospel of Jesus Christ. This code fostered a culture in which white people's sensibilities and comfort were placed ahead of ensuring that people of color didn't experience racism.

I couldn't stay in a community where there were more consequences for speaking up against racism than there were for doing racist stuff, nor could I remain in a place where Black women (or anyone, for that matter) could experience such harsh treatment. Furthermore, I couldn't stay in a church where a pastor would prevent church leaders from providing care to people who were hurting and where his own misdeeds were covered up and relegated to conversation for those in power while the needs of the people most affected by his wrongdoing were ignored. You have to be able to read the room and know when it's time to leave a situation that is no longer life-giving.

Even though it was the right thing to do, the decision to leave Living Streams left me with a profound sense of loss. I wept over the loss of my spiritual home (as dysfunctional as that home was at times). I lamented that the church's culture caused me to worry about getting too close to other Black people out of fear that people's perceptions of me could hurt others' reputations. I grieved that my talents were put under a bushel in order to cater to white people's sensibilities. I even mourned the people who never spoke to me again after I left.

When you start pushing back against racism, several things happen. People who are invested in maintaining the racist status quo rush in to tell you that you're wrong. People will try to police your tone and accuse you of creating division. People will say that they "agree" with you but that they think there's something wrong with some aspect of your advocacy. People will take what you have to say personally and push back. People will take what you have to say personally and quietly see themselves out. Rarely, people will take what you have to say to heart and allow the truth to set them free. With each of these responses comes the potential for loss.

You will lose people who wish to maintain the status quo because they are uninterested in the deep change that is required to make a more just world. You will lose people who accuse you of creating division because they have already sided with injustice and want to feel good about doing so. You will lose people who take issue with your advocacy because you will never fit their agenda. You will lose people who take what you have to say personally because they are unable to recognize that collective healing requires collective responsibility. You may even lose people who take what you have to say to heart because being set free is a process and sometimes folks aren't ready to stand in the truth that they know.

You will lose some people after intense discussions and wrestling over what is right. You will lose others after they decide to silently exit your life. It can hurt just as much when they silently exit as it does when they fight you, in case you're wondering.

Where there is loss, there is also the need for loss management.

Loss management is exactly what it sounds like: managing losses. Every person who exits our lives after deciding they cannot journey with us as we seek deeper levels of liberation is a loss that needs to be managed. Every institution we can no longer be part of due to our commitment to being free is a loss that needs to be managed. Every door that closes in our face because we choose to use our voice is a loss that needs to be managed. I talk about loss management mostly in terms of the interpersonal losses that happen because those are the most acute losses. When we lose our connections to institutions, jobs, communities, and other such affiliations, we are losing the people as much as we are losing the "thing." Even losses that seem insignificant contribute to a constellation of harms that can compound over time.

The first component of loss management is what I refer to as assessment. This is the time where we assess the loss and what damage has been done. During assessment, we take the time to understand what hurts and why it hurts. Do you consider the loss to be major or minor? What are the implications of the loss? Are there relationships, commitments, or affiliations that will need to be examined in light of the loss?

During assessment we triage our wounds, tending to the most serious first and then working our way to the superficial wounds. There might be some urgent decisions that need to be made or actions that need to be taken. You will need to figure out what requires immediate attention and what can wait. You do not have to rush to make any big decisions. It is natural to feel hurt, disoriented, and like your world is falling apart. Take time to sit with the loss and with your feelings about the loss.

The second component of loss management is recognizing and validating grief. Sometimes we compartmentalize the experience of grief to death, but grief can happen over anything. Every loss we experience is a type of death in which we mourn what we had and grieve over what could have been. It is common to experience grief when we lose friends, communities, opportunities, safety, and assurance.

Like I said earlier, racism is theft. It is okay to mourn the things that racism has stolen from you. It is okay to grieve losing things that held importance to you at some point. It is okay to grieve who you were or who you might have become if things were different. It's okay to hold your grief and to carry it along with you in your journey.

Sometimes we feel silly for being sad that we've lost relationships that were toxic or one-sided. We might be well rid of certain influences in our lives, but that doesn't keep the process of losing from hurting. Recognizing and validating our grief requires us to acknowledge it and tell ourselves it is okay to grieve. Grief isn't just about crying; it can show up as anger, bargaining, depression, denial, shock, and other emotions. These feelings can come in cycles, they can be delayed, or we can experience them in waves as they ebb and flow through our lives. There comes a point when we eventually accept what has happened, but it doesn't stop grief from visiting us from time to time.

Grief, for me, has been a constant companion on this journey. It may not be this way for you, but it is true for me. There are times in which I have held grief close like a wise old friend whose presence I wished to savor before they departed to destinations unknown. I have allowed the anger in, singing angry songs and punching the air as I cursed everything and everybody who caused me to hurt. I have danced in the rain of my own tears. I have been too weighed down by grief to move, let alone get out of bed.

Other times, I have tried to run from grief only to be overtaken and felled like a hollowed old tree under the axe of a lumberjack. Every time that I have run from grief, I have regretted it because it has always caught up to me. There have been times when running was necessary so that I could complete time-sensitive tasks. Other times I have run because I haven't wanted to feel the ugliness of my losses. I haven't wanted to remember the feelings of rejection and the ugly things that people have said to me.

Sometimes, grief takes me by surprise and I find myself reeling as I decide how to respond to it. The name of a contact in my phone, a birthday reminder on my calendar, pictures in my photo album, or a video from a festive event are all grief mementos that can take me by surprise. Sometimes checking up on a friend I haven't heard from in a while and finding an "Add Friend" button speaks of that person's silent exodus from my world, and I wonder what I said that triggered it. Sometimes, a sudden, angry message or email lets me know. Other times, seeing people talk bad about me by name in mutual friends' comments sections tells me everything I need to know.

It has been much easier to hold grief close than it has been to run from it. Running from grief isn't running from what is hurting you; it is running from yourself. No matter where you go, you can't get away from yourself, so you might as well learn how to live with yourself instead of running. Our losses become part of us, but they don't have to overcome us. Time can heal our wounds, if we let it. Scars can tell the story of a past battle, a sudden injury, or the precise excision of a malignant growth. Whatever their source, scars tell the story of an injury that was given the needed treatment and time to heal.

The third component of loss management is meaning making. In this context, meaning making is the work that we engage in to help us understand losses that stem from finding our voice. Meaning making doesn't require us to revisit the gory details surrounding our losses (unless doing so will be cathartic and not devolve into dwelling on things that cannot be changed); it can simply involve sitting with the feelings and impressions we have as a result of our loss and discerning what positive things we can gain from them.

As we make meaning of our losses, we can ask ourselves some important questions to guide us along in this process. What does this loss say about this person/institution/community and their commitment to antiracism? In what ways was this relationship preventing me from using my voice? In what ways does this loss motivate me to continue using my voice? In what ways can my faith/spirituality/personal consciousness guide me to a higher understanding of this loss? What spiritual/intellectual resources can I draw from to help me better understand this loss? Are there any significant reorientations or adjustments that I need to make to my life as a result of this loss? What lessons have I learned?

Different losses require a different level of meaning making. Some losses might require extensive processing and significant time spent meaning making. Other losses might require only a shoulder shrug and a "Don't let the doorknob hit cha where the good Lord split cha" before you can move on.

Meaning making is more than simply saying, "Everything happens for a reason." I don't believe that's true. Some things happen for absolutely no good reason. There's no good reason for people who purport to care about us to fail to see us in the fullness of our being and then discard us when we stick up for ourselves. There's no good reason for people to insist on saying, doing, and believing hurtful, demeaning things. There's no good reason for injustice in the world. Instead of saying, "Everything happens for a reason," we can identify the constellation of harms that have led us to this place of grief and loss. Identifying the constellation of harms allows us to do the liberating work of constructing a meaning that gives our loss purpose. And where no purpose can be found, we can still be set free by the wisdom that we have gained.

Meaning making is a deeply personal experience. Others can't make meaning for you, but they can help you find meaning. As you are able, discuss your losses with close friends, mentors, or your therapist. Allow others to help you find meaning in your losses. There are no right or wrong answers, and there is no right or wrong meaning. Our understanding of the meaning of our losses may evolve over time. As we gain more information and mature in our own self-understanding, we might find new meaning in old occurrences.

The fourth component of loss management is boundary setting. Know what your boundaries are when it comes to interacting with people that you have left on read or let go of altogether. Do you have an open-door policy in which anyone can reenter your life at any time? Do you have a closed-door policy in which people must knock and you decide whether they get to reenter? Do you have a locked-door policy that requires specific actions to reenter? Do you have a slammed-door policy in which if the door was slammed upon exit (either by the person or you), there is absolutely no chance of reentry? Do you have a combination of some or all of these?

It is important to set boundaries so you can know what you will do if and when certain situations arise. Sometimes we are forced to revisit our losses when we unexpectedly encounter people who have exited our lives. Sometimes we are confronted with our losses when we have to interact with institutions or communities that remind us of our grief. Sometimes lost opportunities come back around and we must decide how we will engage. If you have decided what you will and will not do ahead of time, it takes away a lot of the stress of having to decide in the moment. And if you make a different decision in the moment, knowing your boundaries will help you reorient yourself and find peace with your decision because you already have some idea of what you will and won't do.

You have the agency to decide whether and how you wish to interact with the people, places, institutions, or communities that caused you harm. Set boundaries that make sense to you and provide for your specific needs. Don't allow yourself to be guilted into entering contested space or interacting with people who have done harm to you if that isn't what you want to do. You do not owe people the privilege of your presence nor are you required to absolve people of their sins against you. You can keep it cute or you can pay them dust. Healing is for you to work through at your own pace. There is no prescribed timeline for healing, and no one can dictate what healing looks like for you.

I am very tenderhearted and struggle with the idea of people being angry with or misunderstanding me. Setting boundaries is how I protect myself from being taken advantage of, apologizing for things that I don't need to apologize for, or remaining in (or reentering) toxic spaces with people who care more about their own sense of dominance than healing. I will accept any genuine attempt toward reconciliation and healing, but the door becomes locked to anyone who feels the need to dump their feelings on me instead of approaching me like a human being. We don't have to agree, but I refuse to be treated like an object.

The last component of loss management is aftercare. Aftercare is the ongoing work that we do to care for ourselves after we finish assessing the loss and tending to our immediate needs in the wake of the loss. It will look different depending on the impact of the loss. For a relatively minor loss, it might look like treating yourself in some way and having a vent session with a friend. More difficult losses should be managed with the help of a qualified mental health professional whenever possible.

When you engage in aftercare, do what will bring you the most peace and joy. Write in your journal (or start one). Engage in meaningful spiritual practices. Spend time with friends and family. Treat yourself to a meal at your favorite restaurant. Go shopping for a new pair of shoes. Volunteer some time with an organization or donate to a worthy cause. Wear your bonnet (or durag) and grease your scalp. Get a massage. Write about the experience in detail and include your feelings. Create something.

Aftercare isn't about escaping from reality, adopting maladaptive coping mechanisms, or overindulging our senses so that we don't have to deal with our pain. It should help us deal with our feelings, not avoid them. It is where we can use our imaginations to envision and create a better life after our loss. Aftercare is what we do to tend to our healing and ensure that we heal properly.

I wish that seeking justice and liberation didn't also come with loss. I wish I could have had a different outcome with every institution, community, and friend that I've lost along the way. I wish more people could have made the journey with me. But in the midst of loss, I still hold out hope.

I hold out hope that one day, something will click and people will do the work of repairing their fractures with me and make amends. I hope that people will one day decide to do right by me and that my cause will be vindicated. At the same time, I have made peace with the presence of grief and loss on this journey. I have gained way more than I lost. For every loss that I've experienced, something better has come into my life.

I lost one spiritual home, but I gained several more places that I count as spiritual homes. In fact, I don't just have spiritual homes; I have spiritual mansions. Places that are full of light and hope with people who see me in the fullness of who I am. I have lost friends and communities, but I have been blessed with more friends and stronger communities.

The losses that I have experienced on this journey of finding my voice have been just as instructive to me as the books I've read, the seminars I've attended, and any other means of knowledge acquisition I've engaged in. The difficult road I traveled has led me exactly where I needed to be exactly when I needed to be there. I don't know if I will ever stop grieving certain losses, but I do know that those losses and their accompanying grief are tools I have used to stage my own liberation. You can use the ashes you hold from your grief to paint a beautiful picture of life and liberation.

17

WAITING TO EXHALE

Longing for Freedom in an Oppressive World

There are two songs that, when I hear them, make me instantly think of my mom and aunties. The first is "Stop in the Name of Love" by the Supremes, and the second is "Exhale (Shoop Shoop)" by Whitney Houston.

"Stop in the Name of Love" makes me think of Mom and my Aunts Donnie, Sue, Becky, and Marsha pretending to be The Supremes in my Aunt Mil's front yard when they were kids. I don't know if they actually did that, but I have a faint memory of them freaking out when they saw old footage of the Supremes on a Motown special back in the day and so I figure that it's possible.

"Exhale" makes me think of them as women in their late thirties and early forties—it's weird to think of them as being my age—and how, when this song came on, they would shake their heads knowingly and sway their hands above their heads, giving the occasional snap or clap on the beat. You know, that Black auntie sway we all seem to pick up somewhere in our thirties when our "song" comes on and everybody knows that it's our song because we are sure to shout to no one in particular, "That's my *song*!" (The song that does this for me is "They Don't Know" by Jon B—only God can judge me.) Even my Aunt Mil, who was nearly twenty years older than Mom and the rest of my aunties, would get in on the moment, her head bobbing just a little bit.

When I look back at that time, it seems like there was something electric about the moment when the movie *Waiting to Exhale* came out. Mom felt that I was too young to see it at the time, but I remember when she watched it, and I remember how it seemed to resonate with the Black women in my world. *Waiting to Exhale* and the song "Exhale" seemed to create a space for Black women where they could be seen and where they could move through this world a little bit freer, knowing that somebody out there saw them in their struggle. This is the essence of liberation: being seen in the fullness of who you are and being free to love and express yourself in a way that brings light and life to others.

As you find and grow into using your voice, remember that liberation is the goal. Allow your voice to be the thing that speaks life over others and brings them into the light of freedom.

Over the years, I have had many interactions with Black people, particularly Black women, who find themselves exhausted as they struggle under the weight of racism in their day-to-day lives. They feel the weight of systemic racism as they attempt to get jobs, obtain an education, and ensure that their families are safe. They deal with interpersonal racism as they navigate various leadership and social roles.

The lexicon that they use to describe their situations includes the words exhausted, fatigued, and worn-out. They are also stressed, frustrated, angry, annoyed, pissed off, hurt, wounded, and upset. But the most common word that I hear is *tired*.

Black people, as a collective, are tired, and we receive little respite from the effects of racism. The myriad sources of pressure and harm that we encounter daily are enough to crush a person. When you add in the impacts on our physical, spiritual, and emotional health, it is a miracle that any of us are still in the land of the living.

Black people are tired, and we don't get no rest.

We are waiting to exhale.

In addition to telling me how tired they are, most of the Black people I interact with say that they are thankful for opportunities to gather with other like-minded Black folk. I have had the privilege of being part of and organizing intentional spaces for Black people where we can talk about our experiences without having to self-edit or where we can just kick it and forget about our cares for a while. In almost every single one of these spaces, the underlying sentiment has been, "It's so good to find out that I'm not alone."

I firmly believe that the Black community and our connection to one another is what has helped us to persevere thus far, and it is what will help us to overcome. We need each other, and we should work to build one another up. Some of us are still on this earth because our connection with other Black people made space for us to exhale.

As we work to build one another up, we should make sure not to leave people out. If our freedom comes at the expense of the most vulnerable people in our communities, then we are not truly free. Freedom that is gained at another person's expense isn't freedom; it is just diverted oppression. A lot of people who say they want freedom really just want to cosplay as oppressors by excluding and harming the people they believe are beneath them. We don't get free by lording our power over others. Freedom is a collective endeavor that requires us to imagine a different world than the one we presently inhabit. As we imagine freedom, it is critical that we imagine freedom for *all* people.

In Black freedom, there is no place for gendered oppression, homophobia, religious violence, classism, ageism, ableism, and any other -ism or phobia that pushes people down instead of lifting them up and inspiring them to become the best version of themselves. Freedom should uplift people. Freedom should galvanize people to break off every weight that encumbers them and release them to flourish. Gaining our freedom doesn't mean we live in a utopia that requires uniformity. Freedom gives us the resources to navigate our differences, use healthy conflict as an opportunity for mutual growth, and strengthen our bonds to one another.

Some people get wary when folks talk specifically about *Black* freedom because they assume that Black freedom means oppression for everyone else. They assume Black people want to continue the same destructive culture that whiteness built, but to do it with Black people hoarding all the power. I'm sure there are Black people out there who want to do exactly that, but most of the folks I talk to just want to live in a world where their body isn't a site of oppression. Black freedom is a specific brand of freedom because Black people have experienced a specific brand of oppression from which we need to be liberated. Freedom isn't exclusive, but it does require us to think in terms of people's specific experiences and needs.

Tending to the specific needs of people in our communities means we should work together instead of competing with one another. There is enough freedom to be had for everyone. Black people have been so put down and abused by society that there are times when we compete for resources when we should be sharing and cocreating with one another. Freedom isn't a commodity that can be rationed, and so we shouldn't approach it from a mindset of scarcity. Anything that purports to be freedom but only belongs to a certain group or can only be attained by amassing power over other people isn't freedom.

When I envision Black freedom, my mind almost always goes to Park Day. When I was growing up, the Black community in my little town held a yearly event the first weekend of August that was formally known as Emancipation Days, but we called it Park Day. During Park Day, Black people from all around would converge on the tiny little park on the Black side of my hometown for three days of food, music, and fun.

My family always played a part in the festivities, which added to my sense of pride about the event. Uncle Bear always served as the DJ and master of ceremonies for the event. The men from Uncle Pootie's lodge would come from an hour away to sell their famous barbecue brisket. Grandma and Aunt Sue ran a booth selling deep-fried catfish nuggets, ice cream, drinks, and other delicious goodies. Aunt Marsha would sing gospel music at the community church service on Sunday.

I tried to be at the park from the very beginning of the festivities to the very end every single day. As soon as we got to the park, I would find my twin cousins, Kendall and Kameron, and we would run around playing like we didn't have a care in the world. We would beg Grandma to make us root beer floats, and sometimes she would let us fill our pockets with candy. I always tried to get as many blue raspberry and sour apple Blow Pops as I could before my supply got cut off.

There were all kinds of tents and booths that sold Black art, airbrushed shirts, fake Dooneys, sunglasses, and just about anything else you could think of. Sometimes I would tag along with Amy and my cousin Staci as they went shopping at the booths or strategically walked around the basketball court so Staci and her friends could gawk at the shirtless young men from out of town. When I got older, my friends and I would also casually stroll by the basketball court, but all I could think about was how funky them dudes must've been from sweating in the summer heat.

Park Day was the time in my life when I felt the most free. It was *the* thing that my cousins and I looked forward to every year. I'm sure that there were conflicts, but all I remember is good times. I'm sure that there were times when it rained, but all I remember is sunshine. I don't even remember being hot at Park Day, and I know that it was probably close to 100 degrees every single day. If I had to sum up the whole vibe of Park Day, I would use one word: freedom.

Park Day represented the best of what it meant to be Black in my hometown. The park became a sacred space where Black people could get together and share the best of us: our food, our music, our dances, and our ways of being together. The Black people in my town and in the surrounding communities became knitted together, sharing a collective consciousness, collective values, and collective care. At Park Day, there was never anybody to tell us to shut up because we were never too loud. Our skin was never too loud. Our culture was never too loud. Our laughter was never too loud. Our existence was never too loud.

I realize that my viewpoint is highly idealized, but that's exactly why I think it is important to talk about freedom from this perspective. Sometimes we have to embrace the ideal so that we are not heartbroken by the real. As much as it pains me to say it, we have a long road to hoe before we are fully free. It's hard for me to fully imagine what it would look like for Black people to live in a world without racism, but I can remember Park Day.

During Park Day, my little town remained the same as it always was. Black folks were still under the white gaze. There were still racist people living there. Black people in my community were still being ravaged by poverty, food insecurity, and the crack epidemic. But for three days, that park became our haven. It became the one place where we were fully seen and fully known. Park Day allowed us to be the best version of ourselves, even if it was just for a weekend. Park Day was where my little community could exhale.

Perhaps, Black freedom requires us to live in the holy tension of "now and not yet." In the "now," we learn to love ourselves and one another so deeply that our presence with one another creates havens of respite where we can exhale. In the "not yet," we continue seeking justice and refuse to shut up until we have attained the full measure of freedom that is our right and entitlement as citizens of a supposedly "free" nation. By embracing the "now and not yet" tension of our freedom, we acknowledge the vast amount of work that is left to do while also being gentle with ourselves and carving out sacred space for gratitude and joy in the midst of the struggle.

In a world that tries to tell Black people we are too loud, I long for the day when we can exhale and our loudness can shift from a form of resistance to a natural part of our existence. As a self-proclaimed loud Black woman, I long for the day when my loudness doesn't have to be armor that protects me from the fiery darts of white supremacy. I long to just be.

As our journey together comes to an end, I hope that my companionship for this moment in your life empowers you to find your voice in a world that tries to silence you. I hope that, as you find your voice, you will embrace being loud and right. I hope that you will take up every millimeter of space that you can. I hope that you have the wisdom to know when to leave people on read or to let them go completely. I hope that when injustice rages, a Holy Hell No will rise up within you. I hope that when you speak, you are able to keep it real so that the forces of racism and white supremacy tremble. I hope that as you speak, injustice crumbles and falls like pebbles into the sea. Most of all, I hope that when you use your voice, you will speak the truth and that the truth will set you free.

Asé and Amen.

CURTAIN CALL

Acknowledging the Community Who Encouraged Me Not to Shut Up

This project was birthed by a community of people. My hands did the typing, but there were many others who positively influenced what went on these pages either directly or indirectly. If you have ever interacted with me (online or off), shared my content, or engaged with anything I have created in the last decade or so, please know that this book wouldn't exist without you.

The problem with making lists and calling people by name is that we always run the risk of leaving people out. If I left you out, please charge it to my head and not my heart.

Thank you to all of my Ancestors in the cloud of witnesses. It is their strength and wisdom that made these words possible. Thank you to my Elders who trod the stony road for me to be able to put these words on paper. Thank you to the town that raised me and the Black community there that nurtured my earliest understanding of myself.

Thank you, Ben, my love, for being my companion and always standing beside me. This book doesn't make it plain enough, but let the record reflect that you have been my champion every step of the way. Thank you, Ezra and Lysander, for giving me a reason to do this work. Thank you, Bella, for keeping my feet warm during these Chicago winters and offering judgment-free puppy cuddles as I bled on some of these pages.

Thank you to the family who nurtured me in my early years, especially Mom and Amy. Thank you, Dad, for always being so proud of me. Thank you to the rest of my family—aunties, uncles, and cousins—for putting up with my nonsense all these years. Thank you all for your love and support. I love you all.

Thank you, Emily H., who I can feel blushing even now, for being a Facebook creeper and becoming one of my greatest allies and best friends. Thank you for holding my tears and curse words. Thank you for endless red velvet donuts and emotional support lattes.

Thank you to my sista-friends, DeeDee R. and Kristina B., for walking with me as I lived through some of the most difficult chapters of this book. Thank you for your friendship, your late-night chats, and your love and support.

Thank you, Tyler Burns, Jemar Tisby, and Beau York, for taking a chance on me and giving me a platform. Thank you also to the rest of The Witness crew, past and present, for holding me down.

Thank you, my "brothers" Kevin W., Ernest L., and Gabriel G., for checking on me, fighting for me, and sending me links and memes.

Thank you to everyone over the years who has encouraged me to make "Good Trouble," including Dr. Shurita T-T., Monica H., Adrién B., The Black Student Concerns crew at Fuller, Rev. Susan and John S., Vicki W., Anele Z., Marquisa R., the interim board at the GLO Center, the Springfield NAACP, Faith Voices of Southwest Missouri, Mr. Lyle F., Miss Gwen M., Mrs. Cheryl C., Jeanelle A., the PTM and PTM 101 mods, past and present, all the people I've met through the PTM group, the distinguished ladies of BBT, and my neguses in Black Chat.

Thank you to everyone who encouraged me to pursue a writing career and everyone who encouraged me to build a public platform.

Thank you to everyone who read early drafts of this work and provided their feedback, especially Alicia Crosby Mack, Ernest L., Anastasia F., and Adam S., whose early input was vital to helping me refine my work.

Thank you, Big Momma's and Eurasia Coffee, for providing food and fuel for my early writing retreats on C-Street. Thank you, Culture Hotel in Springfield, Missouri, for being the delivery room that birthed the early chapters of this work.

Thank you, Chicago, for being such a beautiful city and a place of respite, healing, and inspiration.

Thank you to all of the churches and pastors who nurtured and supported me as I lived the hardest chapters of this book, including Pastor Christie Love, Pastor Holly Madden, Bob, Scott, Lyn, and everyone at The Connecting Grounds; Pastors Emily Bowen-Marler and Phil Snider, along with the beautiful congregation of Brentwood Christian Church; St. John's Episcopal Church for becoming a haven for my family during one of our most difficult moments, especially Fr. David Kendrick for sitting with me in my pain and affirming God's hand on my life.

Thank you, St. Thomas Episcopal Church, for being a place of healing and refreshing, especially Fr. Fulton L. Porter III, for helping me pray this book through.

Thank you, Erin K. Robinson, for allowing me to use your beautiful piece "We Shall Rise" for the cover of this book.

And finally, a big thank you to Trinity McFadden, Stephanie Duncan Smith, The Bindery, Baker Publishing Group, and everyone else who believed in this project enough to make sure that other people read it.

I would also like to acknowledge the people whose harmful antics are chronicled on the pages of this book. I harbor no ill will and have chosen to view your actions as a gift. You have provided the world with an invaluable resource to all who read this work. I hope that one day, I can write a follow-up story that tells the world of your healing and newfound resolve toward justice seeking. Be blessed.

AMDG

Ally Henny is a writer, a speaker, advocate-minister, and vice president of The Witness: A Black Christian Collective, an organization committed to encouraging, engaging, and empowering Black Christians toward liberation from racism. She completed her Master of Divinity from Fuller Theological Seminary with an emphasis in Race, Cultural Identity, and Reconciliation. She hopes to lead a church someday. Ally has been leading conversations about race on social media and her blog, *The Armchair Commentary*, since 2014, and her posts reach millions each month. She is a proud Chicago Southsider.

CONNECT WITH
ALLY HENNY

Find Ally online at **AllyHenny.com** and at her blog
TheArmchairCommentary.com to learn more about what she's
up to and the intersection of race, culture, faith, and antiracism.

CONNECT WITH ALLY ON SOCIAL MEDIA!

 @TheAllyHenny @AllyHenny @TheArmchairCom

 @AllyHennyPage, @GodTalkWithAllyHenny, and @TheArmchairCommentary

LISTEN TO ALLY'S PODCAST

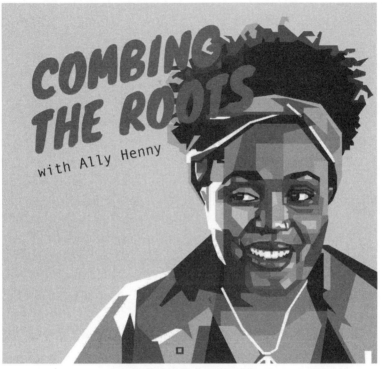

A WITNESS PODCAST

Combing the Roots provides an in-depth look at the issues surrounding racism, justice, and racial healing from a Black woman's perspective. In each episode, Ally explores and exposes the nature of America's race problem, drawing on history, culture, and other sources to provide thoughtful and engaging insight into a deeply contentious issue.

Subscribe to Ally's Patreon at Patreon.com/AllyHenny to get bonus podcast content.

Available wherever podcasts are found.